VII

FOOD PHARMACY

THE NUTRIENT HUNTER

A guide to becoming a nutrient hunter, join the quest to eat our way to better health and a happier planet.

Lina Nertby Aurell & Mia Clase

Photo Ulrika Ekblom

FOOD PHARMACY PRESS®

FOOD PHARMACY PRESS®
Riddargatan 20, 114 51 Stockholm, Sweden
www.FoodPharmacyCo.com

Original title Food Pharmacy Näringsjägaren. En berättelse om hur du curlar planeten och din hälsa genom att ta näringsjägarexamen.

First published by Bonnier Fakta, Stockholm, Sweden.
English translation Cassandra Mechura
Photos By Ulrika Ekblom
Book Design and Illustration Anna Lindelöw Mannheimer
collages by: wellcomeimages.org, rawpixel.com, commons.wikimedia.org
Recipe Developer Therese Elgquist
Editor Linnéa von Zweigbergk
Prepress JK Morris Production
Print Livonia Print, Latvia, 2020
ISBN 978-91-986064-0-9

CONTENT

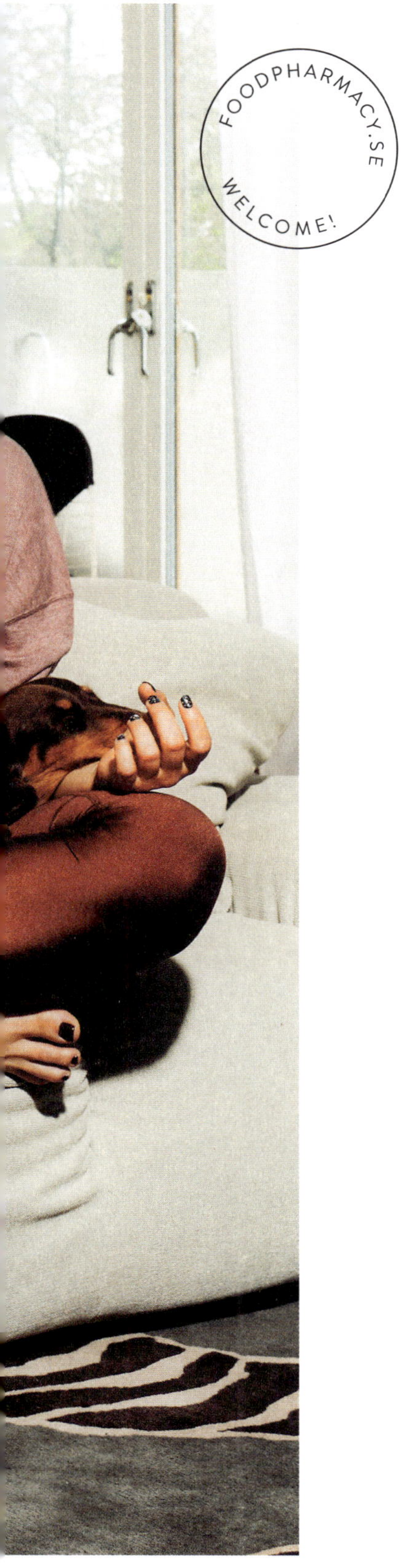

INTRODUCTION MEDITATION

Before we take you along on our expedition through the nutrient jungle, we invite you to enjoy a moment of complete tranquility. Close your eyes and relax your body, part by part, starting from your toes and continuing upwards.

(Well… on second thought, we hope you haven't already closed your eyes, perhaps you should read the following instructions first? When we say "GO" it's time to close your eyes.)

Instructions:
Start by doing a light stretch and find a comfortable position to sit in. Once you've begun by closing your eyes, allow your thoughts to drift among things that make you feel grateful. Then continue to enter a tranquil state by relaxing your body, starting at your feet and working your way upwards. Take an extra second or two to pause on the areas of your body that you are perhaps more critical of. Thank them for always being there for you despite your criticism. Thank the parts you may often take for granted, your heart for pumping the oxygen filled blood throughout your body, and every cell in your body that makes you you.

By practicing gratitude towards your body, you will slowly but surely understand the value of taking care of it. And while you're at it - take a minute to toss some of that gratitude towards our planet, because if there's anyone who is in need of a little tender love and care right now it's our planet.

Okay, you got this. GO.

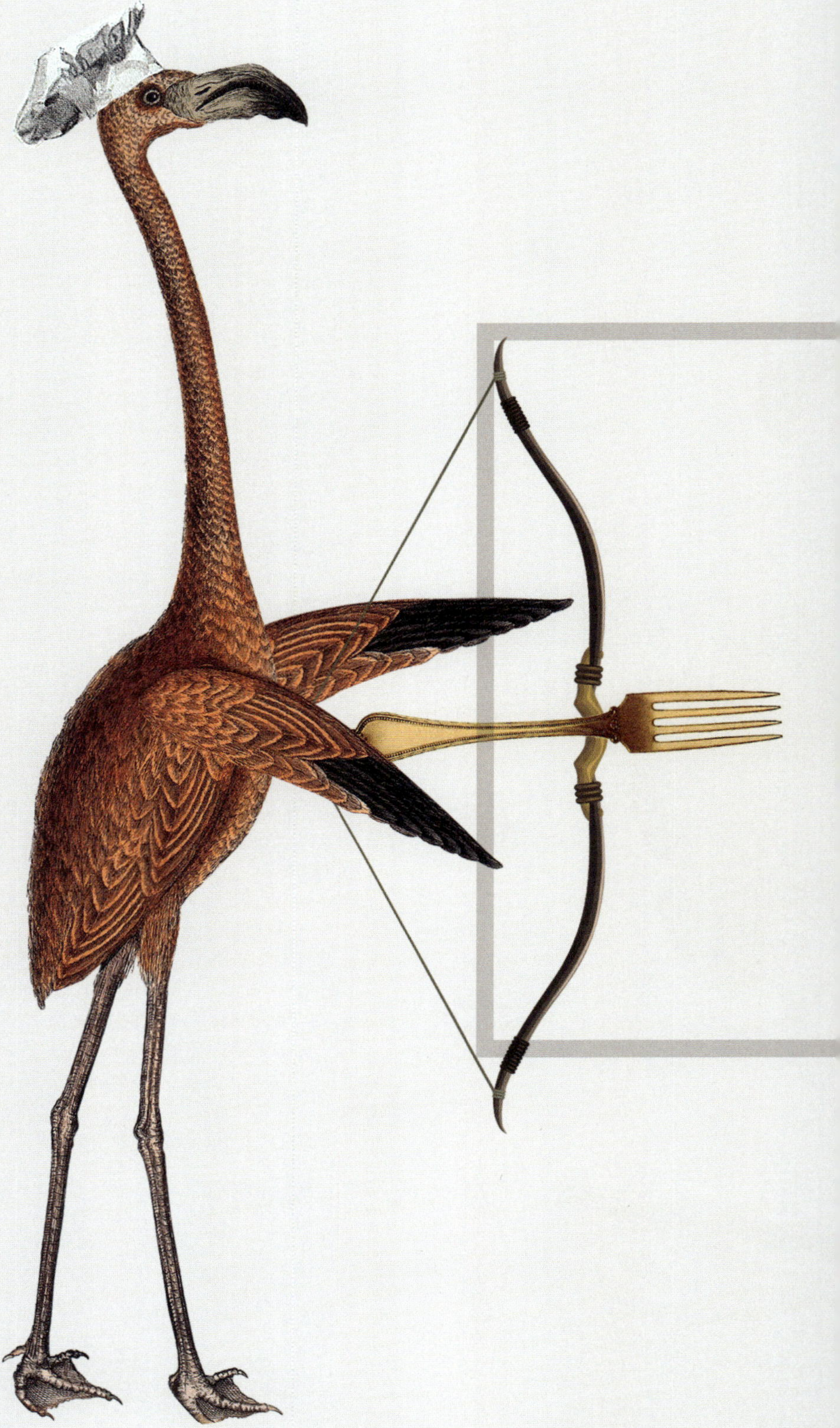

Chapter Nº1

WHAT'S A NUTRIENT HUNTER?

Nutrient Hunters eat with an emphasis on wellness rather than on looking a particular way. Nutrient hunters seek out deeply nourishing food instead of focusing on what to exclude. And although nutrient hunters eat a vast array of foods, they are hunters with great respect for nature.

IMAGINE A CLASSIC WEIGHT LOSS DIET PROGRAM. What comes to mind? We see scales, calorie restrictions, measuring tape, things on a "no" list and in the worst cases, people who eat a particular way not with the intentions to feel their best but to look or live up to a certain ideal. Now, take all of that and throw it in the trash. There are no prohibited items in the nutrient hunter's world and all bodies are welcome! Instead of excluding calories from this and from that, we shift the focus to mindfully selecting nutritious foods and seek out other dietary super boosters, i.e., fiber, antioxidants, vitamins and minerals, as often as possible.

Nice huh? Health is for everyone and not just for a select few with extra time and money. Everyone can be a nutrient hunter - whether or not you visit McDonald's on a regular basis or you have decided to limit sugar consumption to Saturdays, odd weeks or every other year. As long as you make sure there is nourishment in your meals, you can otherwise eat exactly what you want (we would however like to warn you of the likely side effect which is that your body will stop craving junk food as often). Becoming a nutrient hunter is also a win-win for our bodies and the planet. As luck would have it and as if Mother Nature isn't already brilliant enough, the food that is good for us is often also the same food that is kinder towards our planet.

For many, it may feel discouraging to start eating more healthily. We understand the feeling. Before we started our nutrient hunter expedition, we fueled our bodies thoughtlessly with everything we deemed "good" – pizza, burgers, sweetened yogurt, sweetened cereals, baguette with thick slices of Gruyère, french fries, toast with melted butter, sweetened drinks, ice cream, cinnamon buns and other sweets.

Sometimes we'd regret one of our latest gorges and would punishingly starve our bodies for a few days. At the time, becoming a nutrient hunter felt like a long shot. Eating healthy? Ugh, it sounded boring and too idealistic, it was certainly not for us self proclaimed life connoisseurs.

But life works in mysterious ways and once we got a taste of how great we felt after adding a dash more nourishing food to our diets, are eyes slowly opened and we started to see it all from a slightly different viewpoint. Questions like - how wonderful was it really to eat junk if it costs us our health? How long did contentment last after the liter of soda was gone? How awesome was the rest of the day after stuffing ourselves with a bag of candy? Perhaps there was a way to rethink "treating" ourselves, perhaps we could find ways to enjoy treats that didn't mean sacrificing feeling good?

OUR TREK TO BECOMING NUTRIENT HUNTERS

A few years ago, a lot changed in our lives and in order to make a long story a little shorter (though we'll get back to it later) we started to take an interest in our health and we delved into the world of nutritious food. Slowly but steadily our plates went from vegetables playing a supporting role (some days a hardly even visible role), to veggies being the star of the show. This didn't happen overnight though - in the beginning we were content with the replacement of french fries to our burgers with salad and every now and then we tried to bake without refined sugar. The months went by, and one morning we realized that we were no longer actively trying to eat healthy food – it suddenly seemed effortless that the majority of what we ate was nutritious and that the base of our breakfasts, lunches, dinners, desserts and snacks consist of nutritious foods! That's when the idea of being a nutrient hunter hit us.

Nutrient hunter? It all started as a joke that we blurted out during a lecture. But even though we had a laugh at the reference, we felt like that was exactly what we had been for the last five years. Sure, we might romanticize a bit and in retrospect – of course, it's hard to break habits. But in the rear-view mirror, the trek was actually easier and faster than we had ever dared to hope. Along our sometimes very winding path, it has been invaluable to have each other as best friends hand in hand and at times when one of both of us hit one of life's speed bumps, we found the counsel from our dear friend Plato and his first-class theories to provide some guidance.

NUTRIENT HUNTER'S PHILOSOPHY

For those of you who are not familiar with us or Plato, we should inform you that we use Plato's "Theory of Ideas", as the basis for everything we do. Perhaps you find it a bit lazy to simply copy another's philosophy? And perhaps that's true, but Plato's theory has stood the test of time and is perhaps then worth copying. If the theory's doctrine has survived the plague and cholera, the missionaries' crusade in Africa, Europe's Napoleonic era, slavery, the Bolsheviks and ...

Mia looks up from her laptop and makes a time out sign in the air. "That's enough Lina, I think people have gotten the point." Lina rushes to erase World War II and Trump from the document before Mia sees it.

Plato's theory of ideas consists of two parallel worlds: 1) the world of ideal forms (the perfect ideal) and 2) the perceptible world (reality). Simply explained, nothing can exist in reality (the perceptible world) unless there is a perfect idea of it in the world of ideal forms. Still sounding complicated? We'll try to break it down a bit more. In our first book, we used an example of a potato field, but to switch things up this time we can use the Nutrition Hunter Compass.

Imagine you buy a book. In the book you find a practical tool in the form of a nutrient hunter compass that will help you get started tracking your nutrition. The authors write that the compass is based on a perfect ideal of what we should eat more of for good health and to burden the planet less. At first you feel super pumped and vow to follow the compass to the T, but then when reality (the perceptible world) catches up, you are, to say the least, a little frustrated. With stress, family, weekend plans and cinnamon bun days, you succumb to the realization that not everything you put in your mouth now or in the future will not be strictly limited to the Nutrition Hunter Compass.

You now have two choices: to feel unsuccessful or to accept that this is how life is. We suggest the latter. The Nutrition Hunter Compass is just an ideal that you can strive for with your intentions, which is not at all the same as having to follow it to a T for the rest of your life. Use it at your own pace. All quests start at different locations and you yourself set the goals for your journey in becoming a nutrient hunter. And life creates a little push-back, you can always lean on Plato's theory.

NUTRIENT HUNTING WITH RESPECT FOR NATURE

Our quest started out of a desire to improve our health but maybe yours starts due to an environmental interest? When we started to take an interest in what we were putting on our plates, we didn't have a clue that food has as much impact on the environment as it does – for us, environmental awareness was rather about garbage sorting and the transportation sector. But after a few years as a nutrient hunter, the connection between the two issues became more and more apparent to us. Leading environmental researchers advocate that the food most gentle on the environment are the same foods a nutrient hunter's diet consists of. Translation: Nutrient Hunter's food is climate friendly!

SCIENCE FOR YOU

Researchers debate the effect of individual foods and dietary impacts on health but agree on the major points. Our health is rewarded when what we eat largely consists of plant-based food.

But, wait a minute now... Does this mean that the food gives us a chance to influence two of the biggest threats that humanity faces: the global health issues and the climate crisis?

Exactly! But why in the world doesn't everyone know how big of an influence food has on our lives? We asked ourselves exactly the same question and came to the conclusion that no matter how good our governments are or however many medical and environmental journals there are, most of us do not have the time to keep tabs on everything and certainly not to read multiple journals. The knowledge exists - but there is a disconnect between it and the majority of the public. A shame considering how much of an impact we could make starting today.

Imagine if, for example, more people understood the state of public health in western societies and the rate at which it is declining today and that WHO (the World Health Organization) considers food as the biggest culprit of that whole drama. We might then be able to prevent many lifestylerelated diseases. Perhaps if more of us had insight earlier on as to how huge of an impact food has on our planet, and that food production and distribution accounts for approximately one third of the earth's emissions and greenhouse gases, then we might not have come to the point where we discuss things like a planet B. Or as Johan Rockström, one of the world's most prominent professors in environmental science, wisely says: "If we fix food, we will fix the planet. And thus humanity."

Our two heads nodded in agreement as we wrote Rockstöms statement. We don't actually have a second to lose. The knowledge is there and in order to achieve a change it must reach as many people as possible as soon as possible. Hence why we are revealing the Nutrition Hunter Compass in this book. The task of this compass is to make it as simple as possible for you to get as many nutrients and fiber as you can. And as a bonus, all the recipes in this book are climate- calculated to give you a sense of how what you eat affects the climate.

Now that you are on the brink of embarking on one of the most important expeditions for your health and our planet that you will ever partake in, we want to make it as ceremonious as we can for you. Turn the page and whip up a glass of bubbly. Today we toast together for ourselves and for the planet!

PLATONS ELEVATOR PITCH

01. Yes, there is a nutrient hunter compass in the world of ideals that shows how you can eat to care for the planet and your health.

02. Yup, we know that we will not be able to live every day for the rest of our lives in accordance with it (because we live in the perceptible world i.e., reality).

03. But, we will try as best we can!

1 glass

PLATO'S BUBBLY

Here is our best substitute for champagne (Don't get us wrong though, in the real world we love real champagne sometimes too).

sparkling water
1 tbsp apple cider vinegar
or raspberry vinegar if desired
fresh raspberries or strawberries

Mix everything together in a champagne glass and top with a fresh berry. Drink at the same pace as you would drink regular champagne. Cheers!

NUTRIENT HUNTER COMPASS

VOILÀ! In this compass you will find foods that we generally eat too little of and that research data on food and health recommend that we eat more of.

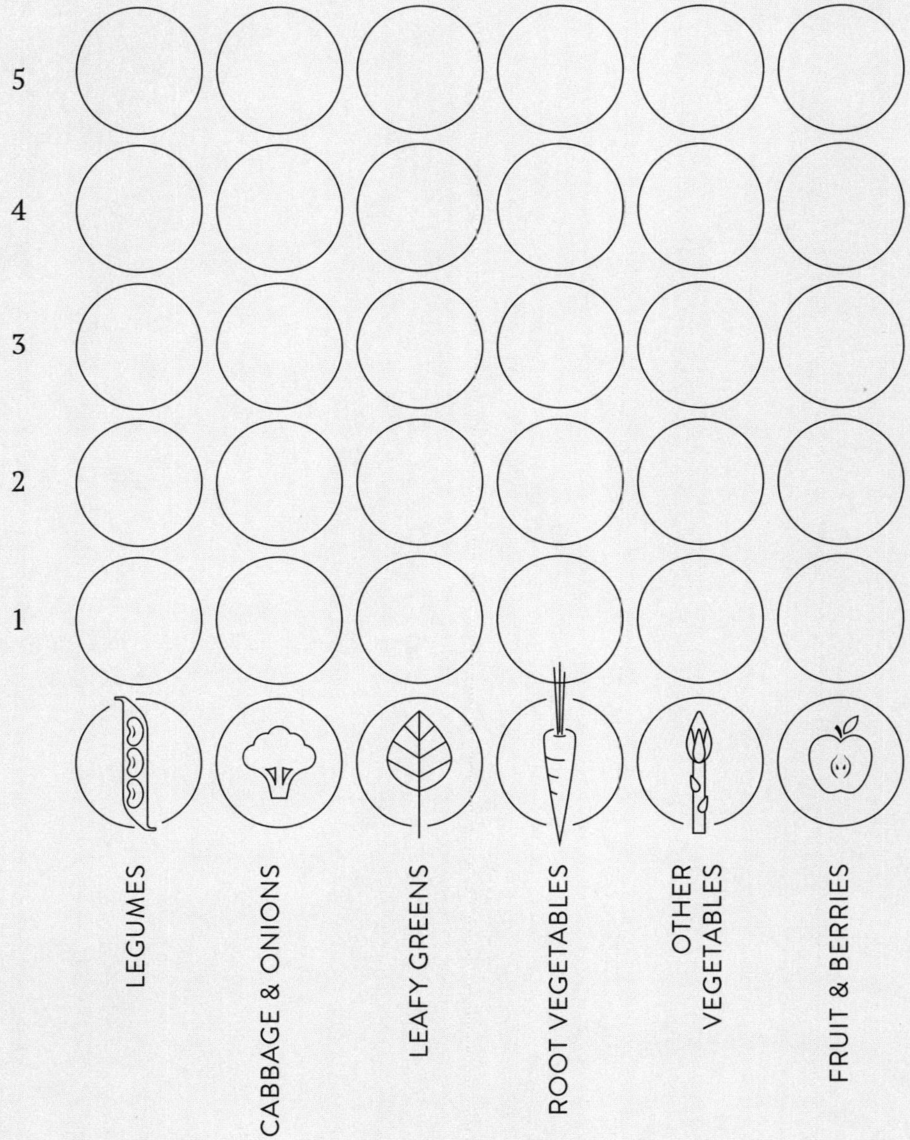

You can find a digital version of the nutrient hunter compass at www.FoodPharmacyCo.com to help you plan meals and provide personal feedback.

HOW TO USE THE NUTRIENT HUNTING COMPASS

The main goal of the Nutrient Hunter Compass is to assist you in achieving a diet that has a wide variety of nutritious foods in many different colors every day and a lot of them. Some call it anti-inflammatory food, others call it gut-friendly and some (we) have gone so far as to call it nutrient hunter food. Whatever you call it, we can state that all food in the Nutrient Hunter Compass is good for our health. As you can see, the compass consists of ten different categories of food, with each category having five circles above it. The circles correspond to one point and the more points you collect per day, the better. Attempt to collect as many points as possible and in the beginning use the compass every day, you will find a digital nutrient hunter compass at www.FoodPharmacyCo.com. Over time, you will get the hang of what a successful nutrient hunter's day in your life looks like and you'll be able to drop the compass and go based on feeling instead.

In order to fill in one point per food category, it is important that you eat a new variant of the food. In order for your expedition to be as simple and durable as possible, it is namely variation that is rewarded in the compass. For example, if you eat broccoli for breakfast, lunch and dinner – then you get a point for broccoli. But if you manage to eat both broccoli, cabbage and brussels sprouts in one day, you can happily tick for three points in the cabbage category. It is built to encourage variety (and to avoid all of the god awful weighing and measuring that is called for in diet programs).

What, that's not fair! Those of you who are a bit more competitive may be thinking. Does that mean that a small little cherry tomato is the same amount of points as a whole tomatosalad? Actually, yes! But with that said, we still want to remind you that it would be wise to put a few extra tomatoes on your plate as long as you have at least one, because then you'll also have a better chance of filling in some gold stars! (What can we say, history repeats itself, you got gold stars when you were young for doing good things and you'll get gold stars now for eating your fruits and veggies. Read more about the gold stars on pages 90–91.)

A bonus from eating food in the Nutrient Hunter Compass is that all your billions of good bacteria in the gut will be in a good mood. Because they feed on fiber which the compass is chalk full of, this means you'll have a strong gut flora (did you know that researchers have found a strong connection between a healthy gut flora and good health?).

In Chapter 4 we will go through the Nutrient Hunter Compass more thoroughly, but you don't have to wait until then to start your journey towards becoming a nutrient hunter. If you are pepped and ready to try, you can start by filling in your most recent meal in the compass and get a better look at your eating habits. You can also try to expand your next meal with as many circles as you can, try swapping every other lunch for a nutrient hunter style lunch or adding more foods from the compass to your everyday dinners. There are many different ways to get started - find the method that suits you best. Remember that the journey should be fun! In the world of nutrient hunters, failures do not exist – for example, if you can't fill in a single circle when you recall your last meal, it's just the way it is and a brilliant way to give yourself incentive to start tracking down where you can get more nutrients into your diet. And if, sorry when, you feel a craving for something that isn't found on the compass, give it a try to do something different from your habits and page through some of the recipe collection further back in the book. With the help of recipes, tips and the Nutrient Hunter Compass, we will keep you company all along the way.

In wrapping up the first chapter we'll give you a glimpse into what's to come. In chapter 2 we'll get to know Anette and her atypical mother, get a recipe for a tasty wrap and better insight into as to why we should get a grip on the agricultural industry and become more conscious consumers. Chapter 2 is all about sustainability and health, but mostly the environment. To be perfectly honest - who has time to care about health and lifestyle-related diseases if the earth's ecosystems are about to collapse?

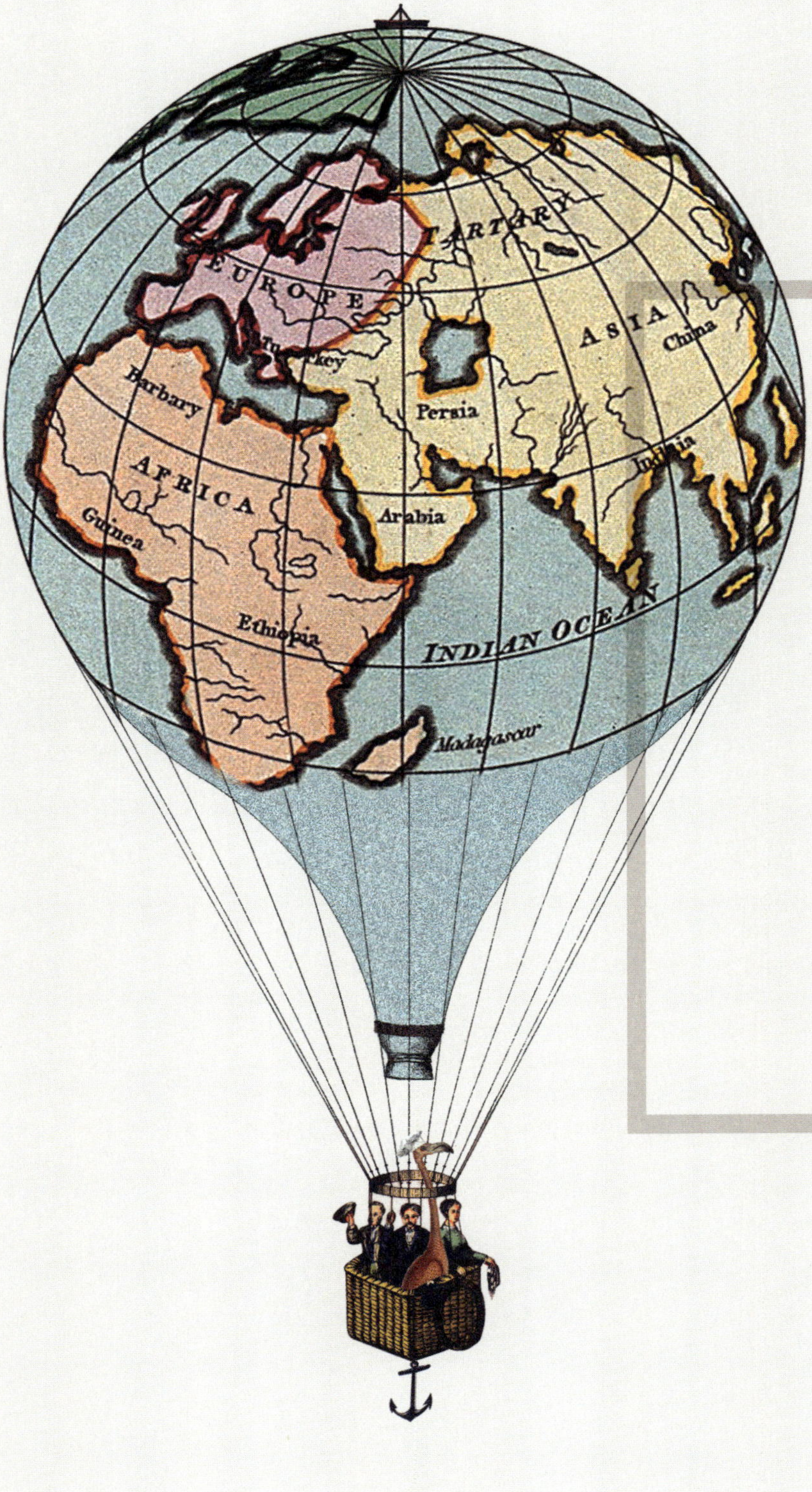
TARTARY
EUROPE
ASIA
China
Turkey
Persia
Barbary
AFRICA
Guinea
Arabia
India
Ethiopia
INDIAN OCEAN
Madagascar

Chapter N°2

THE PLANET

Mother Earth, we hear all too often that you're not feeling so well. This makes us sad. Sometimes everything feels hopeless. What can we do to make you better? Does it even matter if we try?

The simple answer is yes! For heaven's sake, of course it does! Through small adjustments in our everyday lives, we can collectively create impactful change. Simply by making thoughtful selections with our food, we're taking considerably large steps in the right direction. As you'll come to find out in this chapter - not only do we benefit from becoming nutrient hunters but the climate does too! An enormous opportunity to help our planet has been right under our noses.

On our plates.

WHEN WE WERE YOUNG, THERE WAS A GIRL IN OUR CLASS NAMED ANETTE. Anette didn't look like any of the other children. She wore an orange hat, knitted by her mother, and because Anette had an older brother, she usually wore hand-me-down boy clothes. Anette's parents had no car, her mother baked her own sourdough bread, and Anette's birthday invitations stated that she did not wish for any gifts because she cared for the environment and our presence was gift enough.

This was the happy eighties and the beginning of consumption hysteria. Cheap clothes and cheap food made us forget about sustainability. We began throwing away food without so much as a second thought. All the while revelling in the bountiful new phenomena of processed foods that simplified our lives. At times, while sitting at home playing Super Mario Bros and drinking Coca-Cola, we would think about Anette. We would wonder how it was going for her as she protested with her mother in the town square, holding her homemade poster that said, "We only have one planet" and their backpacks packed with homemade sprouted seed bread. It is an understatement to say that we felt sorry for Anette.

Even though this was quite a while ago, the fact is, we still think of Anette. But above all, we think of her mother, Cicki. What a hero! (not to mention, a nutrient hunter long before her time.) Although everyone around her lived in complete ignorance, Cicki never hesitated to stand up for her values and for what she thought was right. At the time, we were glad there was only one mother in the neighborhood who was like Cicki, but today we mourn that there weren't more. Interesting fact: If the world's population lived like the U.S. we would need 5 earths, the EU lives equivalent to that of 2.8, Australia 4.1, the list goes on but you get the gist, we only have one earth so the math doesn't add up here. Imagine if more of us had realized, a little earlier, that we only have one planet. Perhaps then we wouldn't now be discussing where the tipping point of no return is?

It took us a while to open our eyes and see that earth was slowly being pushed towards its demise. In all honesty, we had lived many of our adult years before coming to this realization. Our interest in food started not out of concern for the planet, but out of our personal struggles with health. You see, during the course of a year, we met cancer up close and personal and watched as it claimed the lives of loved ones far too early. Food and its connection to our health became our life's passion, and together we built a new framework for how we want to live and eat.

We wanted to share everything we had and are discovering, so we began our blog, wrote two books and started up a podcast. We traveled high and low and spoke in all sorts of places about the relationship between our bodies and what we eat. One day, an exciting request to be guest speakers presented itself. It was the chance of a lifetime and we felt honoured, we were given free reign as long as we met one small requirement: to include the environment in our lecture. Of course we couldn't say no, but at the same moment that we graciously accepted, we realized the challenge ahead of us. And the more we read through research, the more we couldn't believe our eyes. By golly, food had a much greater impact on the environment than we could have ever imagined! And, hold up a bit now - were we seeing a connection too? Was it possible that the food that is considered the most nutritious is also the food that is kindest towards the environment?

Yes! that's exactly what it was. In fact, the way that we produce and manufacture food today has so much impact on the planet that it deserves a place at the very top of the agenda at the global climate conferences. Does that sound surprising? Let us explain:

FOOD AND THE CLIMATE

When it comes to saving the planet, world efforts have primarily been focused on reducing the use of coal and oil. For example, Sweden's most ambitious climate target has been to become completely fossil-free by 2030 however, meat consumption in both Norway and Sweden have a greater impact on the environment than automobiles. While there has been a lot of discussion about just how much of a burden food and its entire industry has on the environment, facts like this have scientists around the world saying it is high time to align our eating habits with our environmental goals.

In 2018, the journal Science published the most comprehensive analysis of the impact of agriculture on the environment that has ever been conducted. In the analysis, the international research team makes it abundantly clear that the single most effective way to reduce our environmental footprint is to switch to a plant-based diet. According to the research leader, Professor Poore, it is more effective to exclude meat and dairy products from out diet than to cut back on flying or than purchasing an electric car. When we skip a flight or sell our gasoline-driven cars, we only reduce greenhouse gas emissions, while agriculture, on the contrary, is a sector that spans across multiple environmental issues. Cows and sheep release vast amounts of methane, which is a significantly more powerful greenhouse gas than carbon dioxide. The animals waste, manure and feed account for large quantities of emissions. In addition, the majority of livestock rearing, across the globe, is highly inefficient. A completely plant-based diet requires only fractions of the amount of land (approx. ¼ as much) in comparison to the amount of land required to raise all the livestock consumed by the average person in western societies.

What we are about to tell you now sounds absurd, we know. With current eating habits, each person in the U.S. releases an average of 20 metric tons per year, a startling number in contrast to the world average of 4 tons per person. Say though that we were to convert to eating a plant-based diet, we would reduce emissions per person by 72 % from food choices alone. No, you don't need to get new glasses – you read that correctly. Imagine that the only thing required for that drastic a change is that we eat all kinds of delicious foods found on the Nutrient Hunter Compass all the while also supplying our bodies with plenty of nutrients and fiber.

When we consider these figures it becomes quite clear what an enormous burden our meat consumption is on the environment. Without change we are in jeopardy of even more of the earth's population following in the footsteps of the western countries because as far as the rest of the world, statistics show that when a nation's wealth increases, so too does meat consumption. So if meat production and consump-

CLIMATE IMPACT OF COMMON ENTRÉES

Number of kilos of carbon dioxide (CO2 e) per normal-sized portion, source: CarbonCloud

HOW DO YOU KNOW how environmentally friendly a meal is? Well, if you eat plant-based you have nothing to fret over, but it can still be interesting to dig into the details. That's why we have climate calculated all the recipes in the book with the tool CarbonAte developed by the research-based company CarbonCloud in Gothenburg, Sweden. This is their explanation of how it works.

Climate footprints for food show how much a particular food product or dish contributes to climate change. The calculations consist of a database of calculated climate footprints for various food products, developed partly by CarbonCloud and partly by the governmental research institute RISE. The database is built on a large number of scientific studies. Most foods are produced through a process and production chain that contains many different steps before they end up in a grocery store. This chain consists e.g. of production of raw materials for agriculture, followed by agriculture, fish or livestock rearing, transport, processing, packaging and additional transport before the product enters the store. In many cases the chain is long and complicated and in order to calculate a climate footprint in a fair and representative way, all significant emissions along the chain must be included. In order to make climate footprints for different products comparable to each other, it is also important that the calculations are made as equal as possible. CarbonCloud has therefore developed a model tool that consistently calculates all emissions from food production. The tool is based on over 20 years of research about food's impact on the climate and if you are curious to know more you can visit CarbonCloud's website www.carboncloud.io.

How do you know if a meal is climate smart? One way is to take a look at the World Wildlife Fund's (WWF's) recommendation from the One Planet Plate initiative, which set the limit to 0.5 CO_2e.* If you stay under this, you can feel satisfied with your plate. Here in The Nutrient Hunter, all of our recipes are already climate-calculated. !!!

Spaghetti with Ragu Sauce	3,64 CO_2e/p
Beef Stir-fry with Rice	3,04 CO_2e/p
Meatballs with Potatoes and Gravy	4,41 CO_2e/p
Roasted Chicken with Potato Wedges	1,06 CO_2e/p
Macaroni with Hot Dogs and Ketchup	0,57 CO_2e/p
Fish Sticks with Mashed Potatoes and Peas	1,10 CO_2e/p
Salmon With Spinach	1,03 CO_2e/p
Bacon and Hash Browns with Eggs	0,84 CO_2e/p
Lasagna	3,71 CO_2e/p
Cheeseburger with Fries and Ketchup	4,17 CO_2e/p

tion is already one of the biggest reasons for the climate threat today, what happens when countries who have historically consumed very little meat, gain prosperity and begin taking up our meat and dairy habits?

Let's look at this a little closer: Today, people in India eat on average less than 5 kilos of meat per person per year, compared to people in the United States who eat an average of 120 kilos per person per year. If you start to do the math on what happens if the average Indian (population over 1.3 billion) increases its consumption by 115 kilos per person per year to reach the same meat consumption as the average American (population over 325 million), the numbers are dizzying. We believe that a global food revolution is in order. That instead of countries who practice eating largely plant-based diets learning from western societies to over-consume meat and dairy products, it is we who should learn from them and adopt a more sustainable plant-based diet.

A GLOBAL FOOD REVOLUTION

Statistics show that our intake of meat has tripled in the last 40 years. It also shows that as our meat intake rises so does our risk for a variety of lifestyle-related diseases as well. Public health organizations such as The World Cancer Foundation, the World Health Organization and EAT-Lancet Commission recommend that we vary our protein sources (and reduce red meat + processed meats) for a healthier lifestyle. Does this mean that everyone needs to stop eating meat and dairy products completely? Well, for the sake of our health, most of us would be in better condition if we cut down on meat (we promise to return to this in the next chapter). However, we don't have to cut it out completely. The same goes for the sake of the environment, the more of us who give it up, the more the planet will benefit. Worth noting though is that just reducing alone makes a noticeably profound difference.

Some examples:

• If we were to eat entirely plant-based we would reduce our emissions by just over 70 percent, solely through food choices.
• If we skip the meat but continue to eat eggs and dairy products, we reduce emissions by as much as a quarter - from 1.8 tonnes to 1.2 tonnes of emissions per year.
• If we continue to eat meat and just cut out beef (which accounts for by far the largest quantity of emissions), we also come a long way along the path towards a sustainable future.
• Even smaller steps, such as reducing meat consumption by half, are steps in the right direction to reducing our greenhouse gas emissions.

As for what we personally eat and don't eat, we usually adhere to the concept of "When in Rome", we try to go with the flow of whom we are with and where we are (we have no desire to be overly complicated for others). Though that said, in the case of meat, we've almost made it our job to be very particular. Since the variance between good and poor meat quality is vast, we make sure to buy local organic meat from pasture-raised animals. It is better for both the planet and our own health. It also helps to maintain open landscapes and contribute to rich biodiversity. Which in turns means more buzzing bees, singing birds and fragrant flowers!

SCIENCE FOR YOU

Sometimes it can be difficult to find local food, if however, people request local food in stores, it will drive an increase in the demand and thus production of domestic food.

BUT

Worth noting is that local produce is not necessarily more environmentally friendly if the local produce has been grown in heated greenhouses.

LOCAL PRODUCE

Since we've already mentioned local produce a few times, we might as well harp on the fact that it is (most often) a good idea to choose fresh local produce when the opportunity is available. Today, large quantities of food are produced in sensitive tropical zones, which leads to deforestation and a significant loss of biodiversity.

It has also recently been reported that in certain regions of earth where historically a lot of food has been grown, the regions are in danger of becoming unusable due to climate change. This means that the food supply to a country which relies on importing most of what they eat from other countries can become vulnerable. Since an increase in locally produced food is not just going to happen by itself, political platforms need to focus on promoting domestic production - in order for farmers to be willing to make such investments it is necessary that we increase knowledge and awareness and invest in research and support. And, of course, the consumers will have to see the value in paying slightly more for food that is more nutritious and better for the climate.

Eating more local food generally speaking means a reduction in transport, which in turn makes our eating habits more sustainable for the future. Today, transport accounts for about 10-15 percent of the total climate footprint of food. This doesn't necessarily mean that we should completely avoid purchasing produce from other countries though. While this does pose some confusion for us consumers while we meander around the grocery stores, a certain amount of trade is necessary and makes us less vulnerable to situations such as bad harvest seasons (it was actually not too long ago in history that even developed countries like Sweden, for example, would suffer famine after a bad harvest year).

It's easy to conclude that the food industry is complex and that as a consumer it is impossible to keep track of everything, so do not despair if you are unable to find local produce in your store. When shopping for food, we prefer to think in terms of added value. The food we put in our basket should always have some kind of added value. That might mean it is organic, in season, or highly nutritious and sometimes we luck out and strike all of the above.

SCIENCE FOR YOU

Animal welfare laws vary around the globe, buying local meat from smaller farms generally supports higher animal welfare standards.

AND!

Try to keep away from most processed alternatives to meat and invest in raw ingredients instead.

THE PLATE AND THE PLANET

Whether you are 100% meat-free or just cutting back, there is a plethora of climate friendly alternatives. Thanks to the growing plant-based trend, there are countless alternatives that taste as delicious as their classic counterparts. Given the significant role meat plays in environmental stability, we're pretty sure that developments in this area will continue to expand. It's possible that a plant-based diet will soon be the new norm for the majority of society.

ANTIBIOTICS IN MEAT

The global meat industry is considered to be the major culprit behind antibiotic resistance. Namely, two-thirds of all antibiotics are used for livestock. Today, antibiotic resistance is described as one of the most serious threats to global public health. If we do not stop this expansive development, researchers believe that the increase in multi-resistant bacteria will become the most common cause of death in 2050. Meaning that within twenty years, more people will die of multi-resistant bacteria than cancer. Hence, why we nutrient hunters are keen on choosing local organic pastred-raised meat. In Sweden it is prohibited to give antibiotics to live-stock for preventive purposes. In fact, the European Medicines Agency's annual statistics on livestock antibiotic sales indicate that Sweden uses the least antibiotics of any EU country. Swedish-produ-ced organic pasture-raised meat is said to be world-class and more countries could follow suit and improve their antibiotic stewardship.

SCIENCE FOR YOU

Already back in 1945, Alexander Fleming, a Nobel Prize winner who discovered the first antibiotic, warned in an interview with the New York Times about the risk that over-prescribing antibiotics could lead to resistance.

FOR NUTRIENT HUNTERS WHO WANT TO TRY PLANT-BASED PROTEIN

In the past, we did our meal planning based on which animal protein we would be serving - steak, chicken, meatballs, etc. What do you say though? Do you dare to try planning your meals from any of the following protein sources as the base component of your dinner? (If you're not ready to go entirely meatless then start by trying to reduce the animal protein in your menu and increase the amount of plant-based protein.)

Chickpeas
A definite family favorite! Chickpeas are an excellent base for patties of all kinds (well, vegetarian look-alikes sans meat anyways). Season with your favorite spices and freeze them in containers for a ready-to-go meal. Chickpeas can also be roasted as snacks, mixed into salads or puréed into a delectable hummus.

Buckwheat
A plant-based complete protein source. Mix soaked whole grains into a cold porridge, blend up into a smoothie or add some to oatmeal for a hot porridge (see page 121). When soaked or roasted, the grains also become a great addition to use in baking or as salad, soup or smoothie toppings.

Quinoa
A plant-based complete protein source. A satiating high-protein base for salads, patties, soup topping, filling for wraps or as a base in a porridge.

Beans
We love beans in all colors and shapes! Browse the varieties and you will soon discover which ones are your favorites. Soybeans, for example, are one of the most protein packed foods available. You can find them hiding in tofu, but you can also just eat these little treats as they are.

Tofu
As you probably know, tofu needs a bit of tender love and

care, but fortunately it's a simple fix. On page 126 you will find a magic recipe for palak paneer with tofu as an example. And if you crave scrambled eggs for your weekend breakfasts, just let the tofu marinate in tamari before tearing it into pieces and frying it on a low temp. We can attest that it is far from boring!

Seeds

Hemp seeds are yet another plant-based complete protein source. These small seeds are great to sprinkle over porridge or toss into muesli and salads. Fantastic to blend up in a smoothie too! Pumpkin seeds are also a good source of protein. They are extra delicious if you roast them on low heat until they start popping, they'll gain a slightly nutty flavor. And if you've never tried it, we highly recommend blending them up into a beautiful green pumpkin seed butter.

Lentils

No autumn stew is complete without lentils (and actually no winter, spring or summer dish either). If you want a soft start, try sneaking beluga lentils into your regular ground beef sauces or stews. Start light and then increase the amount of lentils while decreasing the meat each time until you've made the conversion over to a fully plant-based recipe. If you season the dish as usual, neither you nor your family members will notice any major difference, we promise!

Once upon a time, at a park in Stockholm, two bikes were lying in the grass next to Lina and Mia who had sprawled out across a picnic blanket for some mid-day relaxation (writing a book is hard work). After a while, Mia dug in her bag and took out a wrap. Lina looked at it hungrily.
Lina, "A wrap, yum!"
"Yes, and this is not just any wrap. This bread is made with potatoes and chickpeas", Mia replied as she poured oat milk in the coffee.
"By the way, I read that plant-based alternatives to dairy products have 70 percent less climate impact than traditional dairy products. What do you think... Could one conclude that all vegan

Darling

4 wraps

CARROT-DOG WRAPS FOR NUTRIENT HUNTERS

Flatbread
See page 140

Carrot-Dogs
8 carrots
4 bay leaves
10 whole allspice
1 ½ teaspoon smoked paprika
1 red onion
salt and freshly ground
black pepper

Mashed potatoes
6–8 potatoes (about 500g)
¼ – ¾ cup oat milk
salt and white pepper

Pickled red onion
1 red onion
1/4 cup water
1 tbsp apple cider vinegar

Pickled cucumber
1/2 cucumber
1/4 cup water
1 tbsp apple cider vinegar

Directions

Make the flatbread according to the instructions on page 140.

Peel and thinly slice the onion, then place in a bowl. Combine water, vinegar and salt and pour over the onion, leave for 30 minutes. Repeat this with the cucumber in a separate bowl.

Peel the carrots and cut off the ends. Bring a pot of water to a boil with the allspice, bay leaves, sliced onion, 1 teaspoon of paprika and salt.

Add the carrots and let them simmer until softened but not mushy. Drain the carrots.

Wash the potatoes and cook them in a pot of boiling water soft enough to mash. Pour off the water and whisk together with the milk, salt and white pepper.

Heat oil in a frying pan. Toss the carrots in the frying pan with the rest of the paprika powder, salt and pepper. The carrot-dogs are ready to serve when they have a browned surface.

Place a dollop of mashed potatoes and two carrot-dogs in a flatbread, then top with pickled red onion and cucumber.

0,1

1 wrap emits 0,13 kg CO_2e

food is better for the climate?" Mia asked
"Nah, it's pretty clear that some plant-based foods have a greater impact on the environment than others. For example, choosing soy drinks grown on rainforest land isn't so good." Lina explained and then continued...
"Either way, research shows that even the least environmentally friendly vegetables create less impact on the environment than the most environmentally friendly meat. And vegetables require less cultivation land and cause lower nitrogen emissions."
Mia unbuttoned the top button in her pants and exhaled. Lina could no longer resist asking,
"Well am I going to get a taste or what?"
Mia reluctantly reached over and handed Lina the smallest piece.

REDUCING FOOD WASTE (MORE NUTRIENTS FOR YOUR BUCK)

Seeing that an enormous amount of time and resources are devoted around the clock to produce food and that this causes great stress on the climate, it is imperative that all food is utilized (sincerely, two former wasters). Did you know, that if food waste was a country, it would be the world's third largest emissions nation? Wow, that means there is a gaping opportunity for improvement, that we can influence and reduce emissions just by saving food from the waste bins! Startlingly, the world's population tosses as much as 30 percent of all food produced straight into the dump. Yes that's true! About 1/3 of the food the world produces is thrown away, equivalating to approximately 1.3 billion tonnes per year. Europe and North America are the worst offenders globally, averaging around 95-115 kg/person annually.

We nearly fell off our chairs when we learned that, that figure also happens to be enough to satiate the entire starving population of earth. This atrocious amount of food waste is not just occurring in our homes but throughout the entire food supply chain, i.e., grocery stores and before the food even reach the stores. A common culprit is food which is tossed simply because it is too ugly despite the fact that it

is still entirely consumable. The loss due to ugly food is greatest amidst root vegetables, vegetables and fruits, where as much as 40-50 percent of everything produced is thrown away. We don't need to be mathematicians or scientists to understand what a waste this is. It becomes especially unnecessary when we consider how easy it is to reduce food waste. Reducing food waste at home is a cinch, and as a double bonus, both your health and your wallet will reward you for taking care of the planet.

Our best everyday tips:

1 Don't buy more food than you need to. It doesn't have to be more complicated than that. Plan your cooking so that large packages are consumed before they go bad.
2 Serve less on the plate. It may sound obvious, but serving smaller portions has proven to drastically reduce food waste. Save leftovers in the freezer or pack a lunch.
3 Utilize the freezer. Keep an eye on what you have in the fridge, pantry and freezer. That way things can be frozen or used before they spoil. Don't forget the often overlooked items like herbs, wine and leftover coffee. Great tip: freeze leftover coffee in ice cube trays. Then put a few pieces in a glass and pour some oat milk over, ta-da! you have a perfect iced latte.)
4 Avoid blindly following the best-by date on the packaging. Keep in mind that the date indicated has a margin of leeway and remember to use your senses, i.e., smell and taste, to determine if the food is still edible.
5 Make use of peels, stalks and cores. Many of us are all too accustomed to throwing these bits out, as with carrots, beets and cauliflower for example, not to mention broccoli stocks. It's a shame since those parts are full of nutrients. Steam them or toss them in the blender and make a good smoothie, soup or dip instead. The same goes for cores and peels.

Of course, we're not implying that you should dismiss the importance of other issues that impact the environment. However, being that our food system is such a heavy strain on the planet, as much as a third of the world's emissions and greenhouse gases, we can't help but stress how simple

DEAR POLITICIANS!

Perhaps it's caught your attention that childhood obesity is officially a BIG issue with nearly 1 out of 4 children suffering. Since junk food advertising targeting kids is linked to increased child weight and obesity we urge you to push the discussion of bans and protect children's health. Though not just for the sake of being a good example, but also due to the enormous financial burden the worsening epidemic of obesity will tax our countries with if we do not make greater efforts to halt it.

And, another thing:

It's not just TV that the kids are watching these days, social media platforms need to be part of the discussion and regulations too. Social media platforms keep large data banks on all users, and the use of children's data to market HFSS [high fat, salt and sugar] food should be included in the junk food marketing bans.

Thank you for your help.

/ Future generations

and smart it is for each of us to create the change needed by adjusting our everyday habits.

What to apply in the perceptible world (a.k.a. reality):

1. The planet would undoubtedly benefit if we used plant-based alternatives for, or at least cut down heavily on, meat and dairy products.
2. As a consumer you can't be knowledgeable about everything. A good rule of thumb is to try to buy foods with "added value", such as organic, local or certified in other ways.
3. As a nutrient hunter, try to focus on what you can include rather than what to exclude. Try cooking a meal using one of the protein sources on pages 30-31 as a jumping point to dive in and try new things!

!!!

This chapter is now nearing its end and it's time to move on to another subject, one that is near and dear to our nutrient hunter hearts, our health. In the next chapter we will get to know the Smith family, we'll learn why it's not enough to continue eating as usual and why telling little nutrient hunter lies is completely harmless (spoiler alert: we call them "green lies" and no, your nose won't start growing).

Chapter N°3

HEALTH

Is it really necessary to become a nutrient hunter? Isn't eating *normal* food enough?

Unfortunately, what we western world countries call *normal*, and eat daily, has changed dramatically over the last few generations. The food we eat today has not only led to an obesity epidemic but also a significant increase in lifestyle-related diseases.

Sorry to be all Debbie Downer but spreading this knowledge is part of the solution, we promise to cheer things up in a bit! In this chapter we'll dive into the food health connection, give you lots of pep, a great smoothie, and teach you the art of charming little green lies.

IF YOU ARE A YOUNG OR MIDDLE-AGED ADULT it may feel frightening to think of possible illnesses and of dying one day. That you will not be there for your child's entire life and that you may never get to see La Sagrada Familia be completed may be disturbing thoughts. Unfortunately, this is, so far at least, the terms of life and something we all have in common. We are born and we die. The only questions unknown regarding death are when and how?

But death doesn't always have to be crushingly sad. For those of us who have had the fortune of an elderly family member in our lives, who lived a full and rich life, but became weary and lacked the zest to go on living, you may have experienced how death can even be longed for. And for those of us who have experienced the misfortune of losing a close relative (hello, beloved mother Lisa, aunt Pia and uncle Kjell, we love you and think of you every day) who left us far too early, know how extremely unfair death can feel. When people who have so much left to give and who are not at all finished with life suddenly die, it can be very difficult to accept that all the years you thought you had left with them are now gone.

Unfortunately, when we first became interested in health, we came to realize that we are not alone in losing close family members far too soon. On the contrary, it seems to be a rule rather than an exception, that there will be someone in your close vicinity who will or has died of a lifestyle-related disease all too young. In fact, lifestyle-related diseases make up the largest percentage of all diseases in the world. Thus, the health problems of the majority of the world's population are largely due to our lifestyle. With all the knowledge we have available to us nowadays, how can this even be possible?

FOOD AND LIFESTYLE-RELATED DISEASES

Let's rewind a few thousand years. If you look at human evolution, then an important survival tactic emerges. As early humans we ate food when we found it - a successful tactic for our species... until now. However, since today's conditions do not reflect those of our ancestors but our bodies still live in accordance to the same laws of nature as they did in Plato's time, our bodies think we have stumbled into a party. Today, food is available just about everywhere, around the clock and in all forms - not to mention that the issue of quantity has flip-flopped as well. We tend to eat too much rather than too little and unfortunately the gluttony is often comprised of foods that deteriorate our health. In fact, the younger generations of Americans are currently predicted to have shorter lifespans than their parents, primarily due to obesity.

Sure, you're thinking, *it's not really news though, American public health has been tipping the scales for awhile? Not all of us are Americans.*

Well, it may surprise you to know that both the U.S. and the U.K. aren't even on the top 10 list of the world's fattest countries anymore. This issue has risen to the level of a global epidemic and is no longer confined to high-income countries. According to WHO, there are now more people who are obese on our planet than who are underweight. The rise of obesity is now affecting every continent except Antarctica (where there are no human civilizations). Sure there are numerous regions with little to no obesity such as Sub-Saharan Africa and parts of Asia, however, these regions also tend to be those with the greatest malnutrition and hunger challenges.

And perhaps now you're thinking, *but how can the picture*

really be this depressing when headlines are always talking about how life expectancy is going up?

You are right. Medical advances are continuously making it possible for men and women to live longer but public health is more complex than just life expectancy. Expansive analysis by hundreds of researchers across 50 countries have revealed a trend that we are living longer, but sicker. Academics and experts use the term "multimorbidity" to describe people suffering multiple (2 or more) chronic conditions and/or diseases simultaneously. Multimorbidity is expected to see a sharp increase by 2035, and life expectancy by that time should have increased by about 3 years. So to translate that, this means that those "extra" years can be expected to be accompanied by multiple health conditions such as, but not limited to, cancer, diabetes, arthritis, dementia, and depression just to name a few.

Mia waves a fly off of her sandwich and while still chewing the previous bite mumbles "Wow, very astonishing numbers"
Lina looked at Mia with a raised eyebrow and a slightly bewildered look on her face, "Astonishing?"
"Not like astonishing in a good way but in an eye opening way, if lifestyle accounts for the majority of all diseases, making many of these diseases preventable, then we have so much to gain by becoming nutrient hunters!" Mia clarified.

There is most definitely a lot to gain from reviewing our eating habits! Lifestyle-related diseases, according to the WHO, account for just over 70 percent of all deaths globally.

In recent years, interest in the impact of food on our health has exploded, and so this got us pondering what the driving force here was. Not long ago, people devoted themselves to diets for cosmetic reasons or to perform better on the track, and now it's all about health, well-being and longevity. What caused this shift?

This is our analysis:

1 The lifestyle-related diseases are spreading throughout modern societies like wildfire. If you haven't yourself been affected then it's highly likely that you know someone who has.

2 There is new research, nearly every day, on the interplay between what we eat and our physical (and even mental) health.

3 These things, combined with the fact that standard health-care primarily focuses on treatment not prevention, means that there is an incredible number of people who are thirsty for more knowledge. People are wondering, "Can I do something, and if so, what measures can I take to secure good health and reduce the risk of becoming ill."

Lina read aloud from her phone, "Wow, listen to this! According to surveys from several western societies like the US, UK and Sweden, more than half of people worry on a regular basis about themselves or someone they love becoming seriously ill."
Mia looked slightly skeptical. "Well, it's not that surprising is it? Both you and I have been concerned about illnesses ourselves."
Lina, "Yeah, but what I was wowing about was the paradox that so many of us are afraid of serious illnesses, yet a large proportion of us are living unhealthy lifestyles that increase our risk of dying prematurely"
Mia frowned, "I suppose the disconnect is that, knowledge about lifestyle and accessibility to healthy eating isn't yet widespread enough.

WESTERN DIETS

We're likely not the only ones who have noticed this but since diets and health have become such a hot topic there are strategies and concepts and advice being given left, right and center, not to mention dieticians or other experts who wrinkle their noses at all of the diets and say, "it's not so complicated to eat healthy, just eat normal foods." The insinuation being that if we just eat as usual, that we would be in tip top form.

Everytime we hear this, we can't help but wonder what their interpretation of normal foods and as usual are? Are they assuming that the dietary recommendations from various national food agencies (which look broadly similar around the world) are the norm for the general public's eating habits and that sticking to that is a good plan? When experts say not to worry too much and just continue to eat as usual, we believe that they are assuming that we as a society already eat according to the recommendations. However, the statistics show something completely different, namely that only a small minority of us eat that way. When we delve into what western societies eat and what they are recommended to eat, there is a large void. We eat too much processed foods and too little of the healthy stuff, this is coupled with most of us being fairly narrow in our selections, and lacking variety in our diets.

Speaking of statistics we took the time to put on our reading glasses (yay for being 40+ !) for this one, an article from Medical News Today highlighting a study published in 2019 in *The Lancet:*

Unhealthy eating is responsible for more deaths worldwide than any other risk factor, including smoking.

We paused our game of backgammon to continue reading:

The Global Burden of Disease Study looked at dietary habits between 1990 and 2017 in 195 countries.
"This study affirms what many have thought for several years, that poor diet is responsible for more deaths than any other risk factor in the world." - study author Dr. Christopher J. L. Murray, director of the Institute for Health Metrics and Evaluation at the University of Washington in Seattle.
An important finding of the study was that insufficient intake of healthful foods could be just as, if not more, damaging than eating too many unhealthful foods.

Some editorials regarding the study state, "the study offers 'evidence to shift the focus' from restricting unhealthful food items to increasing healthful ones.

We forgot about the ongoing backgammon game (probably for the better since one of us is a bad loser, though we won't name names) and started chatting about how completely spot on the Nutrient Hunter Compass was. The entire basis for the Nutrient Hunter Compass is just that - to seek out nutritious foods and get us accustomed to consuming more of the healthy stuff and shift the norms by focusing on inclusion rather than exclusion. "Healthy stuff" are things such as, vegetables, whole grains, legumes, nuts, seeds, fruits and berries (these are the foods we are referring to when we use the term plant-based throughout the book).

THE "AS USUAL" DIET

Let us introduce the Smith family (a.k.a, an average family in any western country). The Smith family is a very ordinary two-child family. Dad, John, is self-employed and Mom, Jane, a teacher. They have a daughter Sarah in preschool and a son Peter in 1st grade.

It's early morning and we are sneaking into the Smith family's kitchen. It is a regular Thursday in April, spring weather has arrived and the family is planning on getting out their outdoor furniture this weekend... BEEP-BEEP-BEEP!!!

Can someone turn off the alarm please?!

John walks into the kitchen to get breakfast started. He takes out a loaf of bread, one of the popular brands from the grocery store. When we look at the contents on the label we see that the bread contains almost as much added sugar as a cookie. Next to the bread, he puts out a box of honey-wheat cheerios and mini yogurts in cheerful colors. They look cute, but their looks are deceiving - sweetened dairy products contain a lot of sugar (some reach almost the same levels as soft drinks) and the amount of sugar in some of the sweetest cereals can be equivalent to that of candy. John presses the coffee maker button which he was wise enough to load the night before and then pours four glasses of orange juice. He clears his throat and hollers to the others that breakfast is ready.

Good morning! Sarah and Peter come down to the kitchen and eat what is served, completely unaware that they will exceed the WHO's health recommendations, a maximum of 26 grams of sugar per day, by the time they are done with their breakfast.

Lina interrupts, "A revamp of the Smith's breakfast really wouldn't be hard at all and they wouldn't even have to miss anything. We could replace the sweetened yogurt with our berry yogurt. The one where we mix bananas, berries and natural yogurt in a blender. And serve it with our granola on page 110.
"Totally!" Mia agreed, "And when it comes to bread, there are so many good alternatives that are easy to bake. Like our seed loaf on page 115. Most kids love it!"
And then Lina replied with what you are probably thinking right now, "The problem is that people don't have time to bake ..."
"Perhaps not on a frequent or regular basis, but making a larger batch and keeping the loaves in the freezer is enough to last for several weeks. For families with children, it's also a cozy activity to do together. Kids love baking!" Mia countered.

It literally takes less than a minute to mix your own berry yogurt and although baking the bread may take a wee bit longer than going to the store to get some, it is a good investment of your time. Eating a breakfast full of nutrients and fiber instead of empty carbs and hopping on a blood sugar roller coaster will set you up for a better more productive day in the long run.

ROOKIE STYLE FOR YOU

If you want to learn more about how food affects the body, then we highly recommend our first book: Food Pharmacy: A Guide to Gut Bacteria, Anti-Inflammatory Foods, and Eating for Health.

TOO MUCH EMPTY CARBS IN "NORMAL" FOOD

Let's continue peeking in on the Smith family's habits. After reviewing their breakfast we can see how a majority of the sugar that the family consumes in a day doesn't come from the obvious sources such as candy, baked goods and ice cream, but rather from what many people refer to as normal food. It pops up in everything from ready-made meals and sauces to yogurt and cereals, all of which contain added sugar. For breakfast, lunch, snacks and dinner, the family also tends to eat lots of something known as empty or refined carbs i.e., food that is poor in nutrition but rich in calories and that behaves in much the same way as regular white sugar does once it is consumed and the body begins to metabolize it (think: white pasta, white rice and white bread). Since this food is high in calories, the Smith family often feels stuffed just after eating, however, soon become hungry again because the food is so nutrient poor which means the body is able to break it down quickly. When you consume a lot of empty carbs it is easy to get stuck in a vicious circle - due to abrupt blood sugar changes, you go from being stuffed to hungry in a short time and despite eating and eating you constantly feel cravings for more food. To top it all off, low fiber food not only makes us hungry more often, it also leaves our good gut bacteria high and dry since most of them rely on the fiber in our diet for sustenance.

"Switching out empty carbs for nutritious alternatives is literally as easy as it gets, you just swap one for another."
"So true! Like using steel-cut oats, quinoa or buckwheat."
"And most empty carbs are fairy flavorless anyways, it's spices, sauces and sides that make a dish delicious."

TOO MUCH SWEET

Before diving deeper into the subject of sugar we would really like to point out that the body has no problem to take care of a cookie every now and then or a piece of chocolate with your coffee. Issues arise when we knowingly or unknowingly bombard our bodies with sweetness overload. Starting the day with a sugarbomb breakfast and following it with an empty carb filled lunch and dinner means all of the body's resources to process "treats" have been expended and the wiggle room is gone.

So just how much sugar does the Smith family consume per year? Well, if we assume that the Smith family lives in the US (although the numbers are relatively similar amongst all western societies), then scientists from the University of

California, whose work focuses around the impact of sugar on health, calculate the average person to consume 17 teaspoons of added sugar per day. This is the equivalent of more than 1 pound per week (an entire standard size bag of sugar from the store per week!) or more than 57 lbs (25 kg) per year. To help you conjure up a visual image of what that looks like, imagine 5 scoops of ice cream with a little chocolate sauce on top every day for 365 days or 3 ½ Snickers bars per day for a year. And the kicker is that those 17 teaspoons are only factoring in the added sugar our bodies are processing, not the natural sugars that we consume through things like fruits, honey, and juices which are also processed as sugar by the body. So the amount we are taxing our bodies with is actually greater.

Mia dug deep into the picnic basket searching for one more marzipan ball, "God they are so good! I can't stop!"
Lina, always quick with a sound comment, '"Well, but it's not really about quitting. It's about replacing sweets with better alternatives, right?"
Mia, while licking her fingers, "Yeah, like these marzipan balls for example".
"Speaking of which, we should put more sweet recipes in the book to help people find better alternatives for treats"
"Definitely!

TOO MUCH MEAT & TOO FEW VEGGIES

Time to get an overview of the Smith family's relationship with meat. Continuing with the notion that the Smith family resides in America, that lands them in the red zone, consuming more than 100 kg (220 lbs) per head annually. While the US and Australia top the charts in meat consumption, Argentina and New Zealand join them at the top as well, and not falling far behind is the majority of Western Europe with averages between 80-90 kg annually. For many of us, the step of giving up meat feels too big, but you don't have to stop overnight or even give it up entirely. A good middle of the road way to get started is to phase out some of the meat in classic dishes. Try adding a bit of beluga lentils to your ragu pasta sauce while reducing a bit of the ground beef, or make a half bean half beef burger, you could also try replacing some of the chicken in a soup with chickpeas as a simple first step. An example of a classic recipe turned plant-based is our stroganoff on page 146, it's made with beans instead of meat.

"Haha, imagine how we would have reacted to that recipe if someone had given it to us ten years ago."
"Yeah, probably not with open arms but we can try to inspire people to take small steps. The trick is to test your way forward. You can start by keeping the meat in the stroganoff and just add a few beans until you get used to them."

When we set out to become more conscious of our meat consumption we stuck to classic recipes. We used the same seasonings and flavors but just altered the animal protein to more plant-based alternatives. Slowly but surely it became the norm for us, and if we so happened to be served these traditional dishes in someone else's home they now seemed to be lacking something - all the extra veggies! Our new found love for vegetables was yet another step in the direction towards becoming a nutrient hunter.

PEPP TIME

Perhaps you're wondering what the point is of dissecting the fictitious Smith family's diet? By looking at the Smith family's eating habits, it becomes clear that when we eat as usual, we are far from eating what various dietary authorities recommend. And unfortunately, there is a risk that reality looks even worse than what the statistics show, since many of the statistics are based on self-reporting and studies have repeatedly shown that people who report what they eat, temporarily hone their habits for the better and omit days when they fall off the rails, like Easter and Christmas.

But don't feel down and defeated now, although the statistics are showing us the ugly truth there is nothing saying we can't change them. The Nutrient Hunter Compass will teach you how easy it is to change. Through simple small tricks your *normal* diet will evolve from an empty carb filled one to a nutritious and fiber rich diet. By replacing the nutrient-poor meals with nutrient-dense alternatives, adding vegetables and using the same seasoning in the dishes, we promise that you won't feel like you're giving anything up, you will feel just as much satisfaction as before (and may we note that that satisfaction usually last longer due to more stable blood sugar). For more inspiration, check out pages 66-67 to see what the Smith family's meal plan looks like after becoming nutrient hunters.

WHERE DID ALL THE NUTRIENTS GO?

Please don't huff and puff and flip the page now as we highlight a few more statistics in the following section. They are a necessary evil to give us perspective on the current situation, what the statistics show is that the average Smith family buys more food per person - which also happens to be more calorie dense - today than their parents did fifty years ago, all while children of today are considerably less active than previous generations. In the Pepp report of 2019 (a survey where 11,000 children participated) the data showed that the majority of children and young people move their bodies too little, eat too much junk food and spend a great deal of their time looking at screens instead of playing.

Only four out of ten children eat vegetables every day, and of those who eat vegetables, the amount consumed is considerably less than the recommended 500 grams of fruit and vegetables per day (a recommended amount by multiple national food agencies). We can't help but think how this might affect the life expectancy of the younger generation. Surely children who are sedentary and have unhealthy diets can not grow up and live long healthy lives? At the very least we know the answer to the equation: sedentary + junk food. It unfortunately leads right down the path to obesity.

We know, we know, here comes the obesity talk again,

but trust us when we say we would rather skip this topic altogether if we could. The whole idea of this book is to help people get off of the diet merry go round. Yet... at the same time, the goal of this book (and everything else we do) is to try and bring this data and knowledge out of the dark and into the public eye, above all, to give you hope of how easy it is to do something about it. And since being overweight and/or obese is one of the indicators that public health authorities use to measure public health, it would be a little strange if we just skipped it.

Let us clarify the following though before we proceed any further on this matter (better to be abundantly clear than not):
When we talk about being overweight and obesity we are never (read: never ever) referring to the cosmetic aspect of the matter. All bodies are equal - tall and short, thick and thin, wrinkled and smooth, black and white. In a nutshell, you are perfect just as you are, there is only one you, so make sure to appreciate your own uniqueness. And in case you've forgotten any of that, then we urge you to flip back to page 5 and thank your body for everything it does for you with our simple meditation. Take your time, we'll be waiting for you right here.

Ok, detour complete. Sorry, where were we? Oh yeah... did you know that obesity is classified by WHO as a disease? And that being overweight is classified as a risk factor for other diseases, particularly cardiovascular disease and diabetes? Obesity has evolved into the world's most common nutrition disorder and WHO frequently discusses matters around the obesity epidemic in their material. Some of what they share are facts and statistics such as: That worldwide obesity has tripled since just 1975 or that 39 % of adults (globally) are overweight and 13 % are obese (as of 2016, though those numbers have likely risen since). Previously mentioned but worth repeating is the fact that the issue is becoming more and more prevalent among our youth. The same statistics from 2016 revealed that 381 million children are overweight or obese. Unfortunately the majority of children school age and up who suffer from being overweight or obese continue

DEAR POLITICIANS!

Using clear *added sugar* indicators on food packages would make a huge impact in helping us to be more conscious of how much sugar we consume. In today's food labels, the added sugar is combined with natural sugars from fruits, berries and vegetables, and it is impossible for an ordinary consumer to know how much refined sugar they are consuming. Let's band together and make better labeling to support better choices.

Thank you for your help.

/ Society

on in life as overweight and obese adults, setting them up for and increasing their risks for all of the associated diseases and potentially premature death.

The simple truth is that obesity has increased dramatically over the last 40-50 years among both children and adults. Only a minority of people in western countries have a BMI under 25 (a classification of normal weight). Scary figures, we know, but without change these metrics will only grow. Although the links between obesity, diabetes and cancer have not yet been fully identified, a large number of tumor and cancer forms are over-represented in the obese, including colon, prostate, breast and endometrial cancers. New research also shows that there is a link between obesity and mental illness, which has seen a dramatic increase in recent years.

Most of all we find it particularly sad that obesity affects children and their futures. By changing our own habits we have a shot at altering the current course. An opportunity to impact generations to come. It may be difficult sometimes to change children's eating habits (we can speak from our own experiences), but the sooner you start the better. Let's take a closer look at an ordinary Monday in Peter Smith's life.

SCIENCE FOR YOU

Type 2 diabetes used to be called adult-onset diabetes because, well, it was something that affected adults. Today, the condition has crept down a few generations due to rising childhood obesity. We now call it type 2 diabetes.

CHILDREN AND "NORMAL" DIETS

Peter has just started first grade. Although he is never very hungry in the morning, Mom, Jane, is always sure to have the kids eat breakfast. So every morning he is offered a sandwich with ham and butter, a small bowl of strawberry yogurt and some cereal. Lunch is eaten at school and consists of something to the tune of white rice, and sweet and sour chicken. Since Mom says that the children must eat vegetables, Peter puts a tablespoon of corn on the plate. After school, Peter goes directly to parkour, his afterschool activity, which is located right next to the school. Jane has sent a snack in his backpack for him to eat after parkour, some cheese crackers and a twinkie. When Peter arrives home, dinner is finished and there are chicken nuggets and french fries which happen to be Peter's favorites. Before Peter brushes his teeth, he realizes that he is a little hungry still. So he enjoys a bowl of instant oatmeal with maple syrup.

The week continues following a similar pattern - chicken nuggets are replaced by hot dogs and macaroni one day and ready-made fish sticks another. On Wednesday, Peter's grandmother picks him up from school and on the way home they buy an ice cream. On Friday it's family movie night with pizza, chips and soft drinks, and on Saturday it is time for weekend brunch with nutella toast, followed by some treats in the afternoon, and after dinner there will be ice cream in front of the TV. On Sunday, Peter will be going to a friend's birthday party, where he will most certainly eat pizza and cake then trolly home with a gift bag of candy.

Looking at Peter's week we get a pretty good picture of what the average child's week looks like in most western countries (figures actually indicate that many children eat even worse than this). In any case, we know for sure that today's children eat too much meat, sugar and empty carbs while consuming far too few vegetables. These are the exact eating habits that WHO, national food agencies and public health authorities warn us can lead to lifestyle-related illnesses and premature death.

Oh no, it's starting to rain and the big raindrops meant their picnic was done.

"This chapter is starting to get a bit heavy, this poor Smith family is being hung out to dry and their futures look all doom and gloom? We're not trying to be the next Stephen King are we?" Lina stated as she ruffled her things together.

Mia folded the picnic blanket together and tucked it in her bike basket, "ha, no, definitely not. This should be a positive book that will give people the push and the support they need to change their habits. It's time to remind them how easy it is to become nutrient hunters!"

"Yes, and we'll need to prepare all the parents out there that Peter might protest when he starts to try new things. A bit like when it's time to wean a baby from their pacifier, you have to persevere and trust that there will come a time when the child doesn't ask for the pacifier anymore."

"True, once Peter has tried something enough times, it won't be

different anymore. And that as a bonus, children who eat a lot of veggies at an early age are more likely to continue doing so as adults."
Lina packs the last things and they jumped on their bikes.

Previously we lived under the assumption that children just naturally prefer hot dogs, pizza and pasta over lentils and brussels sprouts, but then we asked ourselves, is that really true? When we look at children in other parts of the world, we see for example, that there are places where children prefer seaweeds, beans and kimchi. Maybe our kids prefer junk food over seaweed for the simple reason that this is what we teach them to eat?

Between you and us, our children are no different than anyone else's and along the way we have made every mistake you can imagine, we've tried all the tricks and tips and through it all have become a little wiser. For example, we have found that our children automatically eat more vegetables and taste new things if they are really hungry and if there is no other belly filling empty carbs within reach. We realized that all of the little sandwiches here and snacks there we were feeding them were ruining their appetite so that once it was actually dinner they were no longer hungry. Hunger is the best spice and once we understood that, we started to postpone dinner a bit and presented raw vegetables in different colors first and the children threw themselves at them. Well, three out of four anyways (everyone is different).

ROOKIE STYLE FOR YOU

Having trouble getting your kids to eat broccoli? Try chopping up the broccoli stem into sticks and place together with other veggie sticks like carrots.

AND

If your child still avoids the veggies sticks after you've been patiently presenting them for weeks, try putting out a bowl of dip next time!

GREEN LIES

Another thing we learned along the way was how to use green lies to our advantage. Now we know that mothers around the world have warned us not to lie but green lies aren't really lies, not the kind that can get you into trouble anyways, as they are more like secrets. A green lie is something as simple as withholding a vegetablicious fact from your kids when they ask you to cook their favorite food. It sounds something like this:

Child, *"I want pasta for dinner!"*
You, *"Good idea my little darling pie!"*

Then, you make your child's favorite sauce with the exception that this time you add diced onions, broccoli and carrots to the sauce (the pickier your kids are, the finer you'll need to chop, you can even use an immersion blender to remove all evidence).

Green lies work on all sorts of dishes. Leafy greens, which can typically be a little difficult to get children to eat, are perfect to blend up in a smoothie. Start with what your children already like to eat and try to boost the nutrition by adding hidden veggies (all tricks are allowed). Slowly but surely you will notice that your children will get used to new flavors and soon thereafter they will start accepting more new things. The biggest advantage of green lies is that you can say yes instead of no to things that your children request, this makes food and eating more fun for you and your children.

ROOKIE STYLE FOR YOU

Getting kids used to the flavor of dark chocolate can be easier with flavored chocolate like mint. You can also work your way up from 50% to 70% cocoa.

Take chocolate, for example. Imagine that it is a normal day and the children are begging for something chocolate. Instead of being preachy and giving a sermon on why milk chocolate is not good and that they are definitely not getting it in the middle of the week (you know, because you recently became a nutrient hunter), you can just say yes. Just switch out the milk chocolate for a piece of dark chocolate and when you give it to them, make sure to bend down and whisper in their ears - "This is our little secret, don't tell anyone that I gave you chocolate in the middle of the week", and they will skip along happy as a clam.

Same thing works with ice cream. If the kids want ice cream on a Wednesday, you can say: "Hmmm... Okay, why not?" Then you blend up some frozen bananas with cocoa powder or blueberries and top with something the kids like, and voilà instant soft serve ice cream.

The best strategy of turning children into mini nutrient hunters is not to start by removing everything that they like. But instead, start by adding good things into what they already like. And, say yes to unexpected things like dark chocolate on a Monday. The advantage of being a nutrient hunter is that you can say yes to treats with a good conscience!

2 servings

GREEN LIES WITH CAULIFLOWER

½ cup frozen strawberries
1 frozen banana
½ cup frozen cauliflower
1 cup plant-based milk
½ avocado

Textbook example of a green lie. Frozen cauliflower is excellent to hide in an ice cream or smoothie. Frozen parsnips and frozen peas too for that matter.

Put everything in a blender and mix until smooth.

SCIENCE FOR YOU

Avocados are a crop that requires a fair amount of water, in addition they often travel far to reach consumers. So for the sake of the environment, consume avocados in moderation.

QUICK TIP!

We use green lies almost every day. Of course, we get extra satisfaction when we manage to hide vegetables in unsuspected places, like beans in baked goods or lentils in the granola, but even everyday food served at our homes contains many hidden secrets.

In mashed potatoes we usually toss in some sunchokes, or grate cauliflower into our rice and a regular old tomato sauce becomes SUPER tomato sauce once we've added zucchini, lentils and spinach.

0,2

One portion emits 0,2 kg CO_2

THANKS FOR THE TIPS BUT IS BEING A NUTRIENT HUNTER REALLY NECESSARY?

If you feel like 'you got this' then, no, perhaps not. But the reality, which is depicted fairly clearly by a multitude of statistics from around the globe, is that the majority of us haven't got *this*.

Current eating habits = eating too much of nutritionless foods and not enough of healthy foods. In a way, the state of global health is a reflection of all the easily accessible and cheap junk food that our modern agriculture and food industry have created. We started this expedition to change that and would love for you to join!

As previously mentioned many national health authorities recommend that we eat 500 grams of fruit and vegetables per day, unsurprisingly (due to everything we've covered so far) few of us reach that amount. Today, there are numerous studies that show a positive relationship between a large, varied intake of vegetables and good health. A relatively new study from Imperial College in London has measured how our health is affected as we increase our intake of fruits and vegetables. In this study they did not settle for 500 grams but actually measured up to 800 grams (the equivalent of ten fruits or vegetables) and concluded that if we eat 800 grams of fruits or vegetables a day, as much as 7.8 million deaths per year could be prevented. A positive outcome of eating so many plants is that both cholesterol and blood pressure are lowered, some vegetables can even, according to the study, reduce damage to our DNA and reduce the risk of cancer.

SCIENCE FOR YOU

It's worth noting that overeating any particular vegetable, e.g., broccoli, can have a negative impact. Hence why, variation is so important.

Wow! Let's keep reading.

What the study shows is that the closer to 800 grams of fruits and vegetables we come the more our health improves. If you compared eating zero fruits or vegetables to just 200 grams per day then even that small amount of 200 grams reduces the risk of cardiovascular disease by 13 percent. Eating as much as 800 grams of fruit and vegetables a day reduces the risk by 28 percent. Unfortunately, the study only measured up to an intake of 800 grams per day, though many researchers believe that the health benefits would likely continue to increase the more you eat. In fact, there seems to be no real ceiling - so far there hasn't been any research that has shown a threshold (a point at which more plant-based food no longer yields any better health benefits).

Vegetables are full of nutrition, but many scientists actually believe that the most important component of plant-based food could be the fiber. Today, we know that a high intake of fiber prolongs life. At the end of 2018, on behalf of WHO, researchers analyzed a total of 185 previous studies with data on 135 million people, as well as 58 clinical studies with a total of 4,635 participants. According to the researchers, the relationship between health and a high fiber diet is clear: a large intake of fiber can prevent a wide range of lifestyle-related diseases. Fantastic! Fantastic indeed! And yet as many as 90 percent of us in the western world countries eat too little fiber.

But now we are getting a little ahead of ourselves. Backing up a bit, here are some good things to know about fiber:

TURBO FIBER SCHOOL

- Fibers are carbohydrates that cannot be broken down and absorbed by the small intestine. This means that fiber reaches all the way down to the large intestine without any calories being absorbed from them, hence why fiber is not stated as a carbohydrate in the nutritional recommendations of most national health agencies.
- There are two different types of fiber: soluble and insoluble.
- Soluble fiber is found in oats, seeds, beans, vegetables and fruits, among others.
- Insoluble fiber is found in bran, carrot, coconut, cocoa and white beans among others.

HOW MUCH FIBER SHOULD WE EAT?

SCIENCE FOR YOU

If you are currently suffering from obesity and/or type 2 diabetes, fiber can be somewhat of a miracle as it not only keeps us full and satisfied for a long time it also stabilizes our blood sugar.

Ok, so fiber is a good thing, but how much of it should we consume then? Most national health agencies recommend somewhere between 25-35 grams each day, but many researchers believe that we should eat much more than that. When scientists have looked at our ancestors, they estimate that they potentially ate as much as 135 grams a day! But never mind that, the majority of us don't even get up to the 25 gram mark. On the other hand though, research does show that a nutrient hunter (now of course there is no research on nutrient hunters specifically, but on people who eat plant-based food) easily get between 70 and 100 grams of fiber per day. This is good news because a high intake of fiber strengthens your immune system and reduces the risk of many of our most common diseases.

SOLUBLE AND INSOLUBLE FIBER

As you can hear in the name, soluble fiber dissolves in water. Most soluble fibers are also known as prebiotics as they provide food for our good bacteria and help them to flourish and multiply. Many insoluble fibers are also prebiotics but have another important task in the gut: keeping it clean. You could liken the large intestine to a toilet and insoluble fiber to a toilet brush. Every day, the toilet receives new waste (undigested food, heavy metals, pesticides, millions of dead cells and bacteria), it is not very difficult to understand that we feel best when our bodies can remove this waste as efficiently as possible. When we eat insoluble fiber it helps keep things moving along and clean, it can even carry toxins out of the body, in fact, several times more than its own volume.

Lina locked the bike to a lamp post outside her apartment. Mia wiped mascara off her cheeks.
"Many people say that their stomachs can't take too much fiber. Should they just skip it?"
The sky rumbled with a bit of thunder and they hurried inside.

"Well, but research shows low fiber diets can have negative consequences in the long run. Taking it slow and increasing incrementally can help sensitive stomachs make the adjustment."
"Yeah, fiber is such an important cornerstone to good gut health."

In the short term, you can avoid tummy issues by excluding fiber, but in the long term research shows that a low fiber diet has negative health consequences. So, no matter what reason you have to avoid fiber, it may be a good idea to get the help of a dietician to slowly reintroduce fiber into your life.

Prebiotics mean before (pre) life. Contrary to antibiotics which mean against(anti) life.

LIFESTYLE AND WELLNESS GO HAND IN HAND

A wise woman once said that she thought we should start talking about healthy lifespan averages not just average life expectancy. That we should talk about how many healthy years people are living versus just average years of life in total. As we covered earlier in this book, we are living longer but sicker lives. Perhaps a shift in the focus of extending years to a focus on extending the healthy years would improve wellness by illuminating how much lifestyle affects our well being. Our lifestyle has a greater impact on our health than we may have previously realized. Once we ourselves came to the realization that a good lifestyle is the best investment for a long healthy life, we had to find out more.

When we were young, we learned that our bodies are governed by our genes. This is true to some extent. It is correct that we receive a certain set of genes when we are born and that we carry them with us throughout life, but what is incorrect is that we are at the mercy of every gene we have. Today, because of what is known as epigenetics, we know that through lifestyle we can influence whether certain genes are activated or not. So even if you carry less than optimal genes, you can influence them by changing your lifestyle through things such as exercising regularly. Which means, we aren't entirely powerless. This news is both fascinating and fantastic, it has led researchers all over the world to dedicate their careers to studying epigenetic links to everything from cancer and car-

THE SMITH FAMILY BECOMES NUTRIENT HUNTERS

Time to check in on the Smith family and see how simple changes get them onto the nutrient hunter path. At John's job, more people are becoming nutrient hunters and one day John realized perhaps it's time for his family to explore a nutrient hunter lifestyle too. Jane agreed and together they made plans to implement better eating habits. This is what one of their better days looks like:

BREAKFAST

John and Jane find that breakfast is easy to replace. One day they made their own fruit salad with flax seeds topped with cinnamon, and the next granola with natural yogurt and bananas. On the third day they had Food Pharmacy's seed bread. Orange juice is swapped out in favor of an actual orange (which somedays gets tossed in the kids backpacks).

LUNCH

The kids eat lunch at school so John and Jane can't influence their lunch. However, they have talked a lot about becoming nutrient hunters at home. They even agreed to have a little competition everyday to try and collect as many circles as possible in the Nutrient Hunter Compass by adding as many different things from the salad buffet as they can. John and Jane bring a nutritious packed lunch to work everyday, usually leftovers from the night before.

SNACK

John sends Peter with a banana, mixed nuts and a water bottle for after parkour. Meanwhile John and Jane try to turn a new page and find better alternatives than sweets in the afternoon. Many at John's work have jumped on the nutrient hunter bandwagon so he has lots of healthy options. Jane however is surrounded by sweets, so she decides to suggest the idea of stocking healthy options in the breakroom.

DINNER

John and Jane continue to cook classic dishes, to keep the kids interested but add vegetables where they can and replace the rice with things like white quinoa and cauliflower rice. After dinner the family compares their compasses so during dinner, everyone makes a last attempt to get as many circles as they can. They often add things like sliced veggies and hummus or dip and seed crisps.

EVENING SNACK

Evenings are a bit more challenging. Like many of us, they enjoy watching tv shows in the evening and the urge to snack kicks in. But, keeping their compasses in mind, they try to plan snacks that add circles to their compass. Favorites are: oatmeal with seeds, golden milk or a smoothie bowl. Sometimes the kids even request things that they notice their compass is lacking from the day!

diovascular disease to diabetes and depression. Epigenetics, put simply, is the link between genetics and environment.

Being able to take matters into our own hands isn't just important because it is good news for us, it's also an important factor in the pressing issue regarding national economics and healthcare budgets. Would more preventive care reduce the enormous costs our currently unhealthy society is racking up? It would most definitely improve our quality of life but let's get an idea of what costs look like today. In the US, the costs for lifestyle-related and preventable diseases account for more than 75 percent of the nation's healthcare spending (a percent that is similarly reflected in a majority of western countries). Here is a look at some of the costs these diseases incur -

- Heart disease and stroke in the US cost $199 billion per year and $131 billion in lost productivity of healthcare professionals in 2018.
- Cancer care in the US continues to rise and is expected to reach almost $174 billion by 2020.
- Diabetes which can cause, kidney failure, and blindness, along with other medical needs, cost the US healthcare system $237 billion every year.
- Obesity costs the US healthcare system $147 billion per year.

The research is clear, we have a lot to gain by implementing lifestyle changes, even in older age. No matter what your current status or what quantity of junk food you have consumed, it is never too late to make changes that will improve your quality of life. Something that we learned and thought was rather astonishing was that even 70+ year olds can reap big health benefits by changing their lifestyle. And since the majority of the world's population is under 70 that means that the majority definitely have a fighting chance. So come on, time to grab a head of broccoli and get chopping.

BEING A NUTRIENT HUNTER = EATING EPI-SMART

Of course, our lifestyle consists of more than just what we put in our mouths, a whole host of other factors such as how active we are, sleep patterns, whether we stress or smoke, are exposed to chemicals or environmental toxins, even what we think about, how our social life looks and how meaningful we feel our life is, all play a part in our well being. And while we can't control every single minutiae of our lives, establishing good lifestyle and eating habits is an effective way of positively influencing our epigenetic conditions.

One concrete example when it comes to eating habits is diabetes type 2. Today, we know that some people have a greater genetic vulnerability to develop type 2 diabetes than others, nonetheless diabetes type 2 is generally considered to be a lifestyle-related disease. Explained in other words, there are many people who carry an increased risk of type 2 diabetes but who never develop it, while at the same time, someone who does not have biomarkers that increase their risk for the disease may still be diagnosed with it, due to poor lifestyle habits. In addition, there are many people who suffer from type 2 diabetes but can manage their disease and in some cases even completely reverse it and/or go off their medications after altering their diet and lifestyle. There you have it, epigenetics in a nutshell!

CRASH COURSE IN EPIGENETICS

Epigenetics? What does that word even mean? It sounds foreign like Greek or something, and that's exactly what it is. Epigenetics, just like our mentor Plato, is of Greek origin and means "on top of genetics". Genetics is simply the science of heredity and explains why traits such as height and hair color are inherited. Genetics also explains why it is more common for some families to suffer from MS, breast cancer and cardiovascular disease, among other hereditary diseases - traits and predispositions that are innate and passed on from generation to generation through our genes.

Our friend Louise, who is an epigeneticist and researcher at the Karolinska Institute in Stockholm, has taught us that we can think of our genome as a huge encyclopedia. Brilliant analogy by the way! Here's the breakdown of the analogy:
The DNA we have inside our cells is what's called our genome. This genome is what we can imagine as an Encyclopaedia. Just like encyclopaedias have books A-Z, our DNA is similarly organised. Each "book" of DNA is called a chromosome. Our chromosomes are different from one another, just like how book A varies from book Z in an Encyclopaedia set. The text in book A is entirely different than the text in Z though many of the individual words may be the same. Nonetheless an encyclopedia set is not complete without all of the books between A and Z. The same is true for our chromosomes, we must have the entire set of chromosomes 1-23 for a complete genome. And to make things more complicated, we don't have just one encyclopedia set (chromosome set) but two. One set is from our father and the other our mother. And just like you would find similar information within the two sets of encyclopedias, for example if you were to look up tomato in each, you would find two similar but slightly different texts, our DNA from either set varies slightly. Mutations and changes in our genome that give rise to diseases can be compared to spelling errors. All of this complicated stuff makes up you, be grateful for the combinations that make you, you, because unlike encyclopedias there won't be another copy!

Now imagine that Plato is scratching his head. Epigenetics are in fact what has guided his hair cells to become hair cells and not brain cells for example. Thanks to epigenetics and so-called epigenetic markers, the hair cells know which book, which chapter and which page to read when they divide. These different markers can be compared to highlights and they communicate where in the encyclopedia they should read before dividing. In this way, epigenetics has a role in everything that happens within the body, from the moment the egg is fertilized by sperm until we die. And unfortunately, different diseases can occur when highlights are misplaced in our encyclopedia.

How exactly are these epigenetic highlights affected by environment? One example is that some epigenetic markers are affected by the foods we eat, according to a process known as methylcytosine. In order for this process to work as well as possible, we need to eat foods that are rich in folate (leafy green vegetables, for example), or for our gut bacteria to produce folate on their own. The epigenetic process that puts the methyl groups in place can be disrupted if we do not get enough folate, for example, or if we were to endure a high amount of stress for a long period of time, attract a viral infection or smoke. When this process is disrupted, we then risk developing diseases. And this risk is further increased if you also happen to have an innate genetic risk for a particular disease. This is what is meant when it is said that epigenetics are a link between genetics and environment.

Many researchers believe that technology will soon make amazing things possible within healthcare. With the revolutionary technology of the future we will more easily be able to nurture our epigenetic inheritance and we will shake our heads at the time when we only went to the doctor when we were ill. We'll say, " So crazy that people regularly gave their cars a check-up to keep things running smoothly but not their bodies!"

Now that we know that quality of life could be improved for so many as well as a dramatic reduction in premature deaths through lifestyle improvements, we can't wait for a future where healthcare puts more time, energy and resources into helping people avoid getting sick in the first place. However, we shouldn't just sit around waiting for major technological advances or for politicians to reform healthcare. There is already so much that we can do to help ourselves today. So we might as well get started, right!

Being aware of the role epigenetics play in our health is like having a map, and by becoming a nutrient hunter you are also now the proud owner of a compass that will guide you along your journey. The expedition ahead of you is exciting and tasty - changing your normal diet to an epi-smart one is easier than you think. Keep in mind though, it's not about blacklisting everything in your current comfort zone but about making smart additions that benefit you. In return you'll be benefiting your immune system, your family, your friends, the global economy and the planet.

What to apply in the perceptible world (a.k.a. reality):

1. Remember, you are perfect just as your are. Our appearance and bodies differ, that's the way nature works and it's pretty fantastic.
2. Don't go sliding into a dark hole now because you recently realized that you have been one of the Smiths, eating a normal diet and it's time for change. On the contrary, you now have a whole new world to discover! A super-exciting world full of delicious pastas, warm stews, new seasonings, sticky treats, ice creams and savory salads.
3. If you suffer from being overweight or obese, we hope we have managed to open your eyes as to why it may be a good idea to start acquainting yourself with the nutrient hunter's world. Not for cosmetic reasons, but because it increases your chances of living for as long as possible in a strong and healthy body!

In the next chapter coming up we'll share everything you need to know about the Nutrient Hunter Compass - our most important tool as a nutrient hunter. We hope that after completing this last chapter you'll understand why it is a good idea to stop eating as usual and start being on the lookout for extra nutrients. Keep flipping pages(while reading them of course!) to learn more on going bananas with fiber, how to use the compass and why it is so important to celebrate small triumphs along the way.

Chapter N°4

THE NUTRIENT HUNTER COMPASS

Being a nutrient hunter is about getting as much nutrients and fiber as possible in your day to day life. This does *not* mean that you eat nothing other than vegetables nor does it mean that you need to calculate and compare the climate footprint of everything you put in your mouth. We're not extremist. We both have fully functioning social lives, kids and jobs along with all the other things that living in reality entails. The compass is a guide not a bible, it is meant to help you navigate through the good days, bad days and all the in between days.

QUICK QUESTION: WHAT'S THE STORY BEHIND THE NUTRIENT HUNTER COMPASS? Equally quick answer: Nutrients, nutrients, nutrients (and a lot of fiber).

The slightly longer version is that, the Nutrient Hunter Compass bloomed out of a desire to keep tabs on our nutrient and fiber intake, both of which can be found in abundance in legumes, fruits, berries, barley, grains, cabbages, nuts, seeds, vegetables and leafy greens.

NUTRIENT HUNTER COMPASS GOALS

Now that you have understood how vital nutrition and fiber are and that the Nutrient Hunter Compass will help to guide you towards them, you are ready to move on and take a look at the six different guidelines that form the Nutrition Hunter Compass. Our advice to you is to try to keep them in mind, get to know them and soon you'll notice how your awareness will help to guide your choices. Don't stress to learn all of them at once, start with just one or two if that's what you feel comfortable with - it's always better to do what works best for you personally than to follow a template, feel overwhelmed and give up.

!!!

1. Focus on what to include, not what to exclude
2. Fill the plate with as many plants as you can
3. Variation is the name of the game
4. Choose organic, local and in season when possible
5. Eat the whole plant (stems, peels etc.)
6. Cook from scratch

Focus on what to include, not what to exclude

Sorry, but this needs to be repeated over and over again: the key to success as a nutrient hunter is to focus on what you *should* eat, not to obsess over what you should not eat. You should have the attitude that you *can* eat anything, as long as you're making an effort to get as many nutrients as possible otherwise. The Nutrient Hunter Compass will help to keep you full and your blood sugar stabilized. It may take a while to reach the tipping point, but we dare to promise that if you have a little stamina and stick with it, you will no longer have immense cravings, or feel hungry for nutrient-poor empty carbs and junk food. At first, it might seem like an impossible feat - giving up pizza is basically out of the question for most. We get it, we felt the same (but remember what we said, it's not about giving up, it's about getting more of the good stuff), and yet here we are, trying to convince you that soon you won't even miss the pizza. Sure you'll indulge from time to time but the craving for those types of foods will wither over time. It's a bit like ending a relationship that you know is not good for you in the long run - it hurts at first but once your heart has healed you wonder why you didn't end it sooner. That's a bit like how we look at our relationship with pizza and junk food.

The recipes in this book are animal protein free, but you decide over your own plate. Feel free to add meat or fish or to use dairy instead of plant-based milks. See the recipes as inspiration to help you get more of the healthy stuff and take things at your own pace.

Fill the plate with as many plants as you can

When you're on the hunt for nutrients, eat as much as you can - eating large portions of the healthy foods found in the compass is more than okay, it's encouraged! As a nutrient hunter, you never have to go hungry. In fact, plant-based food is a bit of a universal solution. As you increase your knowledge and collect good recipes, you will notice how easy it is to replace sugar and empty carbs, and meat with plant-based alternatives. You will also be surprised how little the dishes differ in flavor.

SCIENCE FOR YOU

Since different types of fiber yield different health benefits, it's a good idea to eat all kinds of fiber from a variety of sources.

Variation is the name of the game

Today, as much as 60 percent of all calories consumed on earth come from only four crops: wheat, rice, corn and potatoes. Three-quarters of all food consumed on earth comes from only twelve different plants and five animal species.

Lots of people love potatoes, and as for fruit, apples tend to top the list and there's no harm in that per se but a one-sided diet is neither good for our health or the planet. This is why variety is one of the benchmarks in the Nutrient Hunter Compass. Different types of plants contain different substances and we humans thrive on having a very diversified diet in order for our bodies to function optimally. Unfortunately, there is no miracle food that contains everything we need - not even large quantities of kale are the holy grail. Research shows that a wide variety of different kinds of raw fruits and vegetables is optimal for our health. It is not yet fully understood how all components of these plants interact within our bodies, only that they do.

SCIENCE FOR YOU

The colors of all fruits and vegetables contain antioxidants in the form of phytochemicals. These act as plants' immune systems, protecting them from UV radiation and attacks by viruses, bacteria and pollutants.

When we eat a varied diet, we consume lots of different colors of fruits and vegetables which is good, because different colors contain different kinds of phytochemicals (antioxidants) that have positive effects on our health. If you only ate red plants, for example, you would only get those kinds of phytochemicals. But if you ate red, green and purple plants, you would get a wider spectrum of the color palette and the bonus is that when different kinds of phytochemicals are combined they strengthen one another. Many antioxidants defend themselves against only specific radicals, so it is important to get a good mix of different vegetables, fruits, berries and nuts, and not just live on carrots and cashews day in and day out. As a general rule, try to get at least three colors from the plant kingdom every time you eat - since the different antioxidants in the colors enhance each other's properties and the outcome becomes 1+1+1 = more than 3.

Choose organic, local and in season when possible

Yes, we know that organic tomatoes are more expensive than conventionally grown tomatoes, nonetheless, despite the slightly higher prices we always strive to buy organic and keep in mind all of the benefits. Want to know why?

Because, there are many health benefits associated with organically produced food, primarily that organic fruits and vegetables contain fewer residues of dangerous pesticides and chemicals used on conventionally grown fruits and vegetables. A committee of the European Parliament commissioned researchers to produce a report on the issue, the conclusion drawn by the researchers was that the chemical residues in conventionally grown fruits and vegetables can pose health risks to those who consume them. Residues from various pesticides can be traced in the majority of us, largely due to all the sprayed fruits and vegetables that we consume. But luckily, research shows that if you switch to organic, the amount of chemical residues traced in your urine decrease significantly within just one week. Good to know!! So try to prioritize organic produce before filling up your basket with extra items that aren't necessary. And now comes a curveball tip, if you find yourself in the grocery store stuck between a rock and a hard place and you can't swing the organic, then by all means choose conventionally grown vegetables rather than none at all. Research has also shown that the potentially negative effects of pesticides never exceeds the importance of regularly eating plenty of fruit and vegetables.

SCIENCE FOR YOU

Unfortunately, the notion that frozen produce is less nutritious than fresh is a widely believed one. However, studies on leafy greens show that the oracle value (antioxidants) is reduced by half just an hour after the leaves are picked. Freezing stops the oxidation process and preserves nutrients for an extended period of time. So if you have more than you can eat, toss it in the freezer to preserve all those antioxidants until another day.

Our best tip for those who want to become a nutrient hunter but are unable to buy organic products is to look for locally grown and in season as much as possible at farmers markets. There are many small growers who are organic but who, due to financial constraints, cannot afford to obtain the certificates required for the labeling. In other words, some fruits and vegetables may lack markings but are completely free of spraying agents. Ask if you are unsure.

When there are no local alternatives for specific items, you can always try to get creative. Take rice, for example. Rice is primarily cultivated in Asia but if we think outside the box, we can find substitutes that are produced and more readily available in western countries. You could try to replace rice with, buckwheat, oat groats or barley (all of which are also more nutritious than white rice) Give it a try, you'll see, it's delicious!

Eat the whole plant

Pre-nutrient hunter, we always threw away stalks, leaves, peels and stems, as we didn't know that they contain lots of important fibers, minerals and vitamins (sometimes more than the vegetable itself). This is also true of fruits - many of us have become accustomed to not eating the seeds and peels even though they contain lots of nutrients. Nowadays though, we make an effort to use the whole carrot, parsnip, apple or broccoli. This was initially primarily for health reasons, but we've come to realize that our new way of utilizing the whole plant is good for the environment as well. Yet another example of how the environment wins when we tend to our health!

The same is true when it comes to empty carbohydrates - most of us are familiar with nutritionless flours, skipping the nutrient-dense germ and bran. In foods that have been processed and refined (i.e. heated and otherwise altered) the nutrients have often been damaged and/or removed and the fibers have been converted to sugars. Purchase whole and as unprocessed ingredients as you can to bypass this whole issue. When it comes to grains, it is important that they are treated as little as possible. The less processed, the better - that applies to both health and the environment. Not only will you get more nutrients and fiber, but you also avoid a lot of unnecessary additives. Also worth noting is to remember to favor smoothies over juices. In a juice, the liquid has been separated from the fiber, meaning a blood sugar spike in most cases. In a smoothie, on the other hand, you have used the whole fruit or vegetable and retained all the wonderful fibers. Smoothies are also a great opportunity to use peels, cores, stalks and stems.

Cook from scratch

We really want to emphasize cooking from scratch (and FYI it is absolutely possible to be a nutrient hunter and cook from scratch without spending much time in the kitchen). For many years, we prioritized efficiency and then ready-made foods entered our kitchens. Nutrition and time together went out the window when we thought everything just needed to be quick. Now, a few years later, we feel like things maybe went a little too quick, and suddenly we long for more intention and meaning. Whether you go with a homemade soup whizzed together in your blender or long cook something for hours, homemade food generally provides more nutrition, fiber and gratitude.

4 servings

VEGELICIOUS GAZPACHO

2 lbs / 1 kg of tomatoes
1 cucumber
1 red bell pepper
2 garlic cloves, crushed
1 small red onion, chopped
2 tablespoons freshly squeezed lemon juice
1 tablespoon olive oil
1/2 package fresh basil
1/2 package of chives
1 package fresh parsley
salt and freshly ground black pepper

Topping
halved cherry tomatoes, finely chopped red onion, basil, parsley and sunflower seeds

This recipe fills lots of circles in your Nutrient Hunter Compass. Each portion contains a daily ration of vegetables (500 grams, the recommended amount of fruit and vegetables per day).

Put everything in your blender and mix until the soup is as smooth as you'd like it to be. Season with salt and pepper. Allow it to stand for a while in the refrigerator before serving. Top with halved cherry tomatoes, chopped herbs and sunflower seeds.

0,4

A 500g serving without topping emits 0,4 kg CO_2e

NUTRIENT HUNTER COMPASS – HOW DOES IT WORK?

Well there you have it, we made it through the compass guidelines. And now we're starting to get a bit hungry so Mia suggested we take a little break and cook up a batch of our new favorite soup that just so happens to contain exactly 500 grams of vegetables per serving. Once you come back and settle down in your reading chair again, we will take a little closer look at how to use the Nutrient Hunter Compass. Sound good?

HOW DO THE CATEGORIES WORK?

Research actually shows that there is a greater chance that new habits will be long-lasting if they are implemented over time and not too abruptly. If your current routine consists of foods not included in the compass, this doesn't mean that you have to change overnight. Much the same as that you wouldn't go from being a couch potato to running a marathon within a matter of days, you do not go from eating as usual to being a nutrient eating machine overnight. Keep in mind that it is always better to increase your intake of plant-based foods slowly than not doing anything at all. No matter where you are starting from, it's up to you. Set your own pace and goals and try to collect as many circles as you can. To make the hunt for nutrients extra fun you could start rewarding yourself with something you like once you've achieved your set goals? Lina imagines something like a massage. Mia dreams of Netflix time.

SCIENCE FOR YOU

No rule goes without an exception - there are plant-based foods that are complete protein sources all on their own, such as buckwheat, hemp and soy.

Legumes
Soybeans, yellow peas, black beans, borlotti beans, beluga lentils, red lentils, fava beans... Legumes are not only good, healthy and full of fiber, they are also a very good source of protein. The most common question we get from people who are new to eating more plant-based is undoubtedly, how they should get enough protein. Especially those who exercise a lot.

NUTRIENT HUNTER COMPASS

VOILÀ! In this compass you will find foods that we generally eat too little of, and collected data from research on food and health recommend that we eat more of.

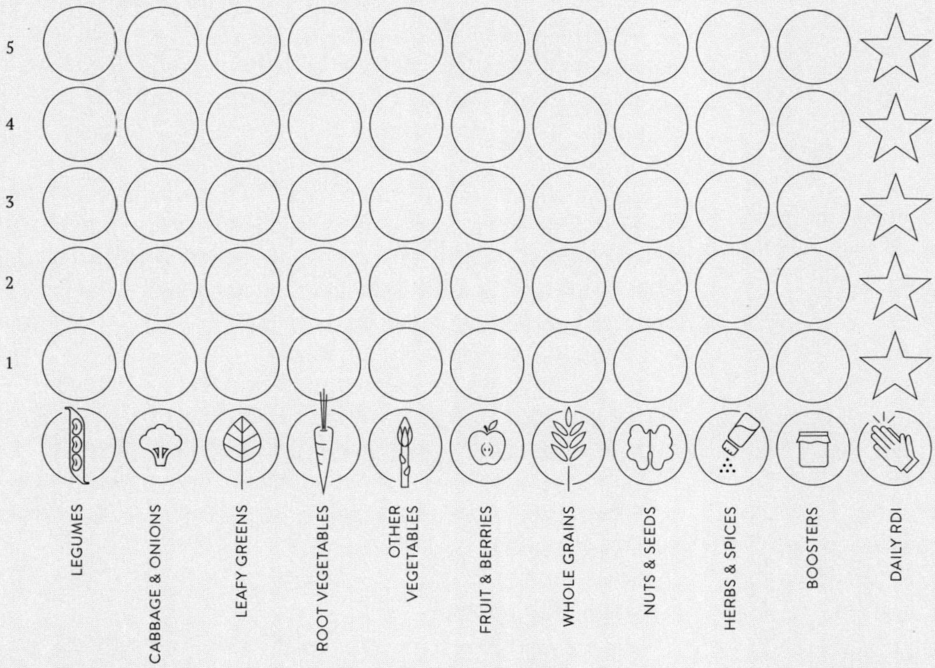

GOALS

1. Focus on what to include, not what to exclude
2. Fill the plate with as many plants as you can
3. Variation is the name of the game
4. Choose organic, local and in season when possible
5. Eat the whole plant (stems, peels etc.)
6. Cook from scratch

Of various plant-based foods, legumes are especially rich in protein. Protein is built up of a total of twenty different amino acids. Although our bodies can produce many of these amino acids, it can't make them all. The 9 that we are unable to produce (known as essential amino acids) must be obtained from food.

In animal protein - protein from meat, poultry, fish and dairy - we find all nine essential amino acids, which is why these sources are considered complete protein sources.

Many plants do not contain all of the essential amino acids and are therefore not complete proteins, but (and listen now, because this is important) as long as we eat a variety of different plants, we can consume all of the essential amino acids we need, seeing as that all nine essential amino acids can be found amongst various edible plants. In this way, protein from plant-based sources can also be complete. In the past, it was thought that the different proteins needed to be eaten during the same meal in order to be complete, but today we know that it's enough as long as you eat them during the same day. The body sorts out the rest on its own!

The only thing you need to think about when it comes to protein is that you meet your basic calorie needs, that is, you eat enough calories per day - this is a basic requirement for the protein to be used as building blocks. If you have a calorie deficit, proteins are used as energy instead of building up and repairing cells.

Cabbage and onions

Cabbage and onions have historically been staples and served at virtually every meal. Both cabbage and onions are available in many different varieties and compliment most anything. They are cheap, filling, healthy and above all, good! Try to eat different varieties of cabbage and onions every day, there is a lot of research that shows that a high intake has a positive impact on health. Onions are a fantastic flavor enhancer and cabbage can replace a lot of nutrient-poor foods in a typical diet - roasted, sauteed, marinated, massaged or smoothie. There is no limit to what you can do with cabbage, it's a great way to get plenty of vitamins and minerals.

A general rule of thumb is that heat destroys antioxidants, however there is one antioxidant called lycopene that is released only when it comes into contact with heat. Lycopene is available in tomatoes and apricots among other things.

Leafy Greens
We love leafy greens! Not least because they contain so much fiber and loads of nutrients. When we started our expedition, we started drinking a green smoothie every day. Not because it was good but rather because it was an easy way to get large amounts of leafy greens into our diet on a daily basis. Today, the relationship is reversed. We now drink smoothies because they are so insanely good and we don't know where we would be without them. Oh, how times change!

Root vegetables
Root vegetables are another great staple - they are cheap and contain lots of vitamins, fibers and minerals. We are aware of the fact that some people chose to exclude foods that grow underground and if you belong to that group you can completely skip this category and focus on filling your circles in the other categories. But, if you belong to the other team who never says no to a potato, carrot or beet, you'll be glad to know you can find lots of exciting nutrient hunter recipes later on in the book. Potatoes may sound boring to some but if you ask your gut bacteria they will tell you that cold potatoes are full of resistant starch which they love.

Other vegetables
This category includes all vegetables that do not belong to root vegetables, cabbage and onions or leafy greens. That means tomatoes, cucumbers, celery and everything in between (yes, yes we know that tomato is a fruit but since it's more common to put it in a salad than a fruit salad we've put it together with vegetables in the compass). This is usually the easiest category to get points in. But remember - there's no limit really on veggies, so you don't have to stop eating just because you have eaten five vegetables in one day.

How you choose to cook the vegetables is entirely up to you. It can be good to know that raw vegetables are often richer in both antioxidants and fiber than cooked. Another tip for retaining the antioxidants is to heat up your vegetables more gently. This means that instead of grilling over high heat or roasting at high temperatures, you can steam, boil or reduce temperatures when grilling or baking.

There's also always the option of combining hot and cold. We often do this with salads, soups and stews. We cook red lentils and onions in a little broth, but before we eat them we pour them into a food processor together with raw vegetables like broccoli and cauliflower and pulse a few times. Or simply cut up a few veggies like mushrooms and onions and put them in a strainer, boil sweet potato or zucchini noodles and when you pour out the cooking water pour it over the mushrooms and onions so they get a light blanching. Then toss everything back in the saucepan and add 1 tablespoon of tamari, 1 teaspoon of sesame oil and a dash of cayenne before stirring everything together. Let it sit with the lid on for a few minutes and serve!

Is it really not possible to overeat vegetables? Well, technically it is but there are only a few rare exceptions. Raw mushrooms are one such example - due to a substance called agaritine, which belongs to a group of chemical substances called phenylhydrazones, you should limit yourself to 100 grams of raw mushrooms per month. Green and/or sprouted potatoes also contain substances that you should avoid. Lastly, though we doubt many people are at risk for over consuming the following, we thought we would round out this paragraph with a warning about brown algae hijiki as it contains high levels of arsenic.

And if you are going to pick your own mushrooms, avoid the poisonous ones. They're poisonous!

Fruit and berries

Our attitude towards fruit is that most of us would feel better if we ate more. That being said, it is important to remember that you should not overeat fruit. When we started our quest for more nutrients were weren't used to eating a lot of vegetables, so we thought it was easier to increase our intake of fruit instead, plus we had read that most people ate too little fruit today and that research showed a positive relationship between those who eat a lot of fruit and had good health.

ROOKIE STYLE • FOR YOU •

Eat plenty of fruit but limit the ripe sweet fruit to a maximum of three per day.

If you eat large amounts of fruit every day, you can try replacing a fruit with a vegetable or at least choose tart fruits (lower blood sugar impact), unripe fruits (more fiber and less sugar than ripe) or berries instead of yellow bananas and grapes. That's what we did and slowly but surely we went on to eat more and more vegetables but nowadays fruit is used mainly as a sweetener when we cook, bake or mix up a smoothie, or as a last minute snack.

By the way, we love berries! And preferably those that we can pick in the forest and gardens ourselves such as currants, blueberries, blackberries, lingonberries, cloudberries, strawberries and raspberries. Berries are excellent as a topping, dessert or snack. Berries are also great to combine with spices and nuts.

Whole grains

For a nutrient hunter whole or coarsely cut grains (such as whole rye, steel cut oats or buckwheat) are an excellent replacement. Did you know that rye, barley and oats are part of a group of grains known as ancient grains? Ancient grains are grains and pseudocereals (quinoa, chia seeds, amaranth) that have been minimally altered by selective breeding since the dawn of the agricultural revolution, in contrast to more common grains such as rice, corn and wheat, which are the result of thousands of years of selective breeding.

For those who want to exclude gluten, quinoa, millet and buckwheat are great alternatives. And if you want to exclude grains and cereals altogether, you can just replace them with vegetables entirely.

Nuts and seeds

SCIENCE FOR YOU

Raw flaxseed contain hydrogen cyanide, which is toxic in excessive amounts, but if you stick to two tablespoons per day, you're safe.

Nuts and seeds are included in the dietary guidelines of countries around the world. Studies indicate that they are tied to a reduced risk of several chronic diseases, including cardiovascular disease, type 2 diabetes, and various forms of cancer. Research also suggest that they positively impact cognitive health, insulin sensitivity, hypertension and cholesterol levels. So how many nuts per day does it take to start to reap some of these benefits you might be wondering? Answer: 30 grams.

It's 8:30 p.m. and Lina has just dozed off when her phone rings.
"Hi! How much is 30 grams of walnuts?" Mia asked
"What?" Lina asked groggily

ANCIENT GRAINS AND GLUTEN

Many people worry that they are eating poorly when they consume gluten containing foods, however, there may be a difference between altered and non altered grains. What exactly do we mean by that? Well, for those who do not suffer from celiac disease (gluten intolerance) it is often no problem to eat whole grains served in their unprocessed original forms.

Gluten is the binder that helps to hold dough together and what creates the elasticity in bread that allows it to rise. In order to produce bread with fast-rising properties, the food industry has altered wheat to contain more gluten. Ancient grains such as rye and barley on the other hand, are not as processed and altered as modern wheat varieties. In addition, they contain a wider array of various gluten proteins, which is believed to lower the risk of triggering an immune system response.

Because gluten is made up of a variety of proteins, researchers believe that varying consumption among the different wheat sorts (which was previously common practice), can contribute significantly to preventing the development of gluten intolerance. In countries such as Italy and Germany, where they regularly consume a variety of local grains, gluten intolerance is not nearly as prevalent as say, Scandinavia, where the proportion of people affected by gluten intolerance is high and variation of grain consumption is low.

Researchers usually measure the effect of antioxidants in something called ORAC (Oxygen Radical Absorption Capacity), which shows the concentration of antioxidants in different foods. Most spices contain large amounts of antioxidants per gram.

Mia, a bit more of a night owl, repeated herself, "30 grams... How many walnuts would that be?"
Lina, "Not 100% sure but about six pieces maybe?"
"Thanks. Nighty night." Mia whispered after realizing she'd just woken Lina.

Walnuts are one of the nuts that has recently enjoyed the limelight thanks to several scientific studies. Since nuts have been shown to reduce the risk of cardiovascular disease in so many studies, the EU Commission, after assessment by EFSA, has decided that a health claim for effects related to cardiovascular function may be made for the consumption of 30 grams of walnuts per day. There is thus a good scientific basis that 30 grams of walnuts per day can reduce your risk of cardiovascular disease, which is a small revolution in and of itself, since cardiovascular disease is the number one cause of death globally.

Herbs and spices

A nutrient hunters spice cabinet is always well-filled seeing as that spices not only add flavor to dishes they are packed with antioxidants, especially polyphenols (a powerful antioxidant). If you haven't yet explored all the many kinds of spices and herbs there are then you will soon find it is like opening the door to a whole other world, one beyond just salt and pepper at least. It wasn't until somewhere around age 30 that we discovered spices were what can take a dish from good to phenomenal. Thyme, turmeric and cinnamon can turn an ordinary eggplant into lasagna, a cauliflower into a "steak" (see page 154) and a date into a cinnamon bun. Speaking of cinnamon, did you know that it can help to stabilize blood sugar!

Fermentation is the process of using microorganisms—yeasts or bacteria—to break down molecules. The healthy bacteria that are present then produce lactic acid, which increases the nutritional value of the food.

Boosters

Boosters increase the health factor of any meal (a meal that consists of pre-made meatballs and pasta easily becomes more nutritious by adding some bean sprouts or kimchi). Fermented, cultured and sprouted foods have a high nutrient density as well as good bacteria. They're a great way to boost your nutrient intake hence why we call them boosters. A few years ago, as a New Year's pledge, we decided that we would try to add two tablespoons of fermented vegetables to dinner every day. In vegetables that have been fermented by lactic acid bacteria you can find all sorts of good healthy bacteria. Just be sure to choose live fermented vegetables from the store and not pasteurized otherwise all of the bacteria are lost. Pasteurization means that the product is processed and many of the beneficial bacteria have died.

How did the New Year's pledge go? We're happy to report, good... deliciously good actually!

Daily RDI

Time to get acquainted with the only column in the compass studded with gold stars. You're already familiar with the recommended daily intake (RDI) of 500 grams of fruit and vegetables as previously discussed, and you remember that unfortunately there are very few of us that reach that amount. Well, the Daily RDI column is for cheering on our nutrient hunters to go above and beyond, you get to collect a gold start for the fruits and veggies you consume beyond the 500 grams. Don't worry, you won't need a scale, it's just about getting a feel for approximately how much 500 grams is. Here is your visual: 500 grams corresponds to two handfuls of vegetables and three fruits or three handfuls of vegetables and two fruits (if you're counting berries as a fruit, a small handful counts as one fruit serving). Research shows that a large amount of fruits and vegetables protects against lifestyle-related diseases and for those who wish to eat more than 500 grams, it's a green light. Reward yourself with a gold star for every extra 100 grams (one handful of veggies or one fruit) you eat after the first 500 grams. Perhaps you were inspired by the results of the study that showed the health benefits of eating 800 grams? Go for it! The researchers behind the study estimate that 800 grams corresponds to about 10 whole fruits and vegetables per day.

ROOKIE STYLE FOR YOU

Even algae, like spirulina or chlorella, can be a booster.

HOW A NUTRIENT HUNTER STAYS PREPARED

In the nutrient hunter compass world, there is no such thing as a mistake (just forget that word all together) but on the days when we have not paid attention to our hunger signals and cravings kick in, the risk is much greater that we eat things that are not on a nutrient hunter's top one hundred list. This is where food prepping comes into the picture - that risk can be minimized by simply anticipating your schedule and habits. You can make it as easy or intricate as you want. Personally we're all about keeping things simple. In our case, prepping has become an increasingly important part of our week's routine, but like the two bohemians we are, we aren't planned and prepped to a T. We do it when we remember and have the time, and the times when we can't, we let things go (though we often regret it since we aren't on our A game then).

Once you've got the hang of things with planning, you'll also notice how food waste automatically decreases. You won't buy a lot of unnecessary things any longer since you have a plan. Plus you'll find ways to use up more parts of the fruits and veggies you buy, because we are eating the whole plant, remember?!

MONTHLY MEGA PREP

If you don't feel like it's your thing to do a little prep every Sunday before the following week, our suggestion is that you start on a slightly smaller scale once a month instead. Here are some suggestions that can be a great help in everyday life. Make it easy for yourself and start with 1 or 2 of the following to begin with.

Make your own spice mixes
In this book you can find all sorts of suggestions from homemade taco seasoning (page 168) to a curry mix (page 169). They are great to have ready for on the fly cooking. It makes for one less step to do while cooking.

Make your own granola
This is easier than you think and you will never regret it. Make a double batch while you're at it and fill a large glass jar so you have plenty. If you think granola is too advanced then you can make it even easier - just mix natural nuts, seeds, grains and spices and pour into a glass jar. Voilà, your own muesli in three minutes!

Bake something sweet
Bake one of our sweet recipes found later in the book (or from the blog) and freeze them in so you have on-the-go healthy treats. A good idea if you know that you tend to have a sweet tooth and a hard time resisting cravings.

Fermented vegetables
Fermented cabbage and other vegetables may not be the first thing you do as a newbie nutrient hunter but once you dare to try it, you'll discover how 1) easy it is, and 2) how practical it is given that fermented vegetables can keep for ages. Here's our favorite recipe:

FERMENTED VEGETABLES

FOOD PHARMACY LOVES

preferred vegetable/vegetables, grated
a pinch of sea salt (or iodine free salt)

Coarsely grate your chosen vegetables and place in a clean bowl. Add a large pinch of salt and stir/work the vegetables for a few minutes until they release some juices. Place in a clean glass jar and pack the vegetables down so that the "juices" cover them. Put on the lid and leave the jar at room temperature (preferably in a darker place) for a few days, or up to a week. Then store in the refrigerator and enjoy.

PREPPING ONCE A WEEK

Food prepping is all about staying ahead of life and preparing veggies to the extent that you basically just need to put a fork in them when it's time to eat. Sure, the nutrients deplete slightly as soon as you cut up fresh produce but if the alternative is that you don't eat it at all then food prepping is always a better option than nothing. Below are our best tips on how to make your hunt easier.

A big batch of soup

Taking the time to make a big batch of soup for the week is a double bonus, the soup can be used for two separate meals. Make a double batch and eat it as soup one night of the week then turn it into a sauce another day or toss in some legumes to transform it into a stew. This way it's not as boring as eating the same soup for several days in a row. On page 133 you will find a delicious recipe that can easily even be tripled.

Prepare some simple breakfasts

Freeze in some ready-made portions of fruits and vegetables? Then all you have to do in the morning is add water, blend and drink a perfect smoothie. Overnight oats and chia pudding are two priceless tricks to add to your repertoire if you haven't tried them yet, double batches here is once again a good idea. Or bake bread and freeze it!

ROOKIE STYLE • FOR YOU •

Have a look at the Food Pharmacy Cookbook for recipes for overnight oats and chia pudding.

Pre-cut veggies

Water is not only good for thirsty humans - veggies love it too and retain their crispness longer when soaked. Keeping pre-cut veggies around makes it a lot more likely that they will get eaten. And adding a bit of water to their container keeps them fresh and crispy instead going soggy. This works for most fruits and veggies actually with the exception of a few like cucumber.

Quick pickled vegetables

Some vegetables benefit from being placed in vinegar rather than in water. Red onion, red cabbage and radishes for example, which we always (read: always when we remember it) cut up and put in glass jars with water and a tablespoon of apple cider vinegar. When marinated in vinegar, their flavor changes (especially onion, which becomes milder), after three days they are perfect. And best of all - now they keep a whole two weeks in the fridge!

Prepare a few salad dressings
May we suggest that you always have a salad dressing on hand? Of course, a flavored vinaigrette works too.

A big base salad for the week
While you're chopping, slicing and soaking vegetables, you can also toss together our coleslaw! The oil and vinegar help this salad to keep all week long in the fridge so you can take it out and serve it as a side to any meal. Feel free to vary the veggies as you please. Keeps well stored in a lidded glass jar.

NUTRIENT HUNTER COLESLAW

FOOD PHARMACY LOVES

Vegetables
250 g kale (regular or tuscan)
1 small head cabbage (white, red or a combo)
3 carrots
1 bunch of celery

Vinaigrette
1 part cold pressed canola or olive oil
1 part apple cider vinegar
salt and freshly ground black pepper

Finely shred the kale and cabbage, grate the carrot, and chop the celery. Whisk together enough vinaigrette for the salad. Massage the salad for a few minutes with the dressing and store in the fridge.

ROOKIE STYLE FOR YOU

Apples that are slightly past their prime can be seeded, thinly sliced with a mandolin, tossed with a sprinkle of cinnamon and baked on a low temp (100°C/200°F) for a few hours to be turned into apple chips. Perfect for Friday night!

Baked or steamed vegetables
On your big prep day, fill a large baking tray with washed

If you want to test a week as a nutrient hunter in the ideal world, it might be a good idea to make it as simple as possible (so you don't get tripped up due to logistics). To lend a helping hand we have created a schedule for you here on the right that you can follow. But by all means, feel free to page through the book and swap out any recipes that you'd prefer.

On the weekends, most of us tend to have a little more time hence why we went with to classic favorites: tacos and pizza. Perfect if you have a partner, children or friends who aren't as gung-ho as you about becoming a nutrient hunter. Everyone can eat the same meal together but choose their sides.

ROOKIE STYLE FOR YOU

For those of you who want to try the ideal world week menu, we suggest that you prepare yourself on Sunday by doing the following:

- Mix the seed and nut mix on page 120.
- Make the coleslaw on the previous page so you can eat it with lunch and dinner all week.
- Cut up different vegetables and soak them in water.
- Make a good dip for your vegetables, like pages 160–161.
- Make some treats so you are ready when a sweet tooth strikes, check out 182–183.

WEEK MENU FOR THE IDEAL WORLD

This is how a weekly menu looks in the ideal world (find the recipes later in the book). Keep in mind that in a completely vegan diet you may need to supplement with vitamin D and B12.

	Breakfast	Lunch	Dinner	Booster
Monday	Seed porridge with tumeric and preferred topping p. 120	Food Pharmacys Golden Soup p. 133	Food Pharmacys Stroganoff, p. 146	2 tbsp fermented veggies + pinch of sprouts
Tuesday	Seed porridge with tumeric and preferred topping p. 120	Stroganoff leftovers	Palak Paneer with tofu, p. 126	2 tbsp fermented veggies + pinch of sprouts
Wednesday	Seed porridge with tumeric and preferred topping p. 120	Palak Paneer leftovers	Gut Loving Lentil-Stew, p. 131	2 tbsp fermented veggies + pinch of sprouts
Thursday	Seed porridge with tumeric and preferred topping p. 120	Lentil Stew leftovers	All-in-one-pan dinner, p. 148	2 tbsp fermented veggies + pinch of sprouts
Friday	Seed porridge with tumeric and preferred topping p. 120	All-in-one-pan leftovers	Food Pharmacys Tacos, p. 149	2 tbsp fermented gveggies + pinch of sprouts
Saturday	Berry Ice Cream p. 111 and White Bean Scones p. 115	Thermos Soup, p. 153	Pizza your way, p. 141	2 tbsp fermented veggies + pinch of sprouts
Sunday	Berry Ice Cream p. 111 and White Bean Scones p. 115	Pizza leftovers	Roasted Cauli-flower Steaks with tahini and tumeric p. 154	2 tbsp fermented veggies + pinch of sprouts

root vegetables and other vegetables that you like to bake (steaming works great too) then keep them in the fridge until later in the week. Eat on top of salads, as a side or to one of the week's sauces as a snack. Some of our favorite vegetables for baking are eggplant, onion, broccoli, zucchini, carrots and rutabaga, but we try to adapt according to season.

Cut the stems
If you buy root vegetables with stems still attached, it can be good to know that cutting the stems off immediately helps the veggie stay fresh longer. What about the stem then?, you ask. Put it in a smoothie, pesto, soup or freeze for another time.

Mini chop veggies for fast cooking
Chopping or slicing vegetables into smaller pieces means that they will require less cooking time when it's time to hit the frying pan or steam basket if that's more your thing.

Soak and pre-cook legumes and grains
Having pre-cooked millet, quinoa and steel cut oats in the fridge is exactly what food prepping is all about! That way they are ready to toss into a soup, salad or whatever. And speaking of pre-cooking, not all grains need to be cooked, take red lentils and buckwheat for example, they are good to go after an overnight soaking, no cooking needed.

NUTRIENT HUNTER GRAIN MIX

FOOD PHARMACY • LOVES •

1 part cooked lentils (beluga/puy/green)
1 part whole grain (oats, barley, millet)
1 part soaked or sprouted buckwheat or red lentils

What you see above is a mix of grains that can stand ready mixed in the fridge and works over a salad, as a soup topping or to blend up and make into patties to name a few of the millions of uses that you could find for it.

DEAR POLITICIANS!

Date labelling systems on food products are confusing for consumers and cause unnecessary waste. The labels range the gamut of, best-by, sell-by, expiration date, best before, end date, maturity date, shelf-life... you get the point.

Creating a clearer more concise system coupled with some campaigning would aid consumers in determining which foods are beyond a safe time frame for consumption and which are merely beyond their window of optimal freshness yet safe for consumption!

Thanks in advance,

Mother Earth

SCIENCE FOR YOU

After soaking buckwheat, it is important that you rinse it properly with boiling water in a sieve to remove the red pigment phagopyrin that can irritate the mucous membranes of the eye.

Sprouting

Not for beginners perhaps but sprouting at home is actually kind of fun, especially for kids and provides the perfect booster. Two beginner sprouts to try are alfalfa and mung beans. There are different ways to sprout, but for people with a tight schedule the simplest way to implement them is to just buy them at the store.

Soak nuts and seeds

When soaking nuts and seeds, it becomes easier for your body to digest and absorb nutrients from them. You can soak the nuts and seeds overnight, cashews, however are best left for a maximum of four hours. Rinse them thoroughly and store in the fridge. Or - dry/roast them at a low temperature in the oven with a bit of salt.

THE RIGHT WEAPONS

ROOKIE STYLE FOR YOU

Rather than freezing in large portions, freeze in portion sizes so things are more readily available. Thawing things overnight in the fridge is a good way to stay ahead.

Unlike a typical hunter, a nutrient hunter does not need a bow and arrows or a gun. A mandolin is of course handy if you want really thin slices of something or a spiralizer if you want to make zucchini noodles. Some glass jars (with clamp lids so you don't have to use foil or plastic) keep the vegetables fresh longer and are kinder towards the planet. A sharp knife or two paired with a couple wooden cutting boards are good basic equipment to have on hand. A large pot and a cast iron pan for all of your veggie endeavours. And if you want to get a bit fancy, perhaps a couple sprouting jars, if you plan to try your hand at that or a steam basket insert if you intend to steam. That list will get you a long ways down your new path but truth be told, beside the knives, you can get along just fine even without all of these things.

ALL ROADS LEAD TO THE NUTRIENT HUNTER EXAM

Every expedition is individual. Take some time to think about what best suits you. Should you start by replacing breakfast, adding nutritious snacks or making sure that each meal has at least three colors? Look through the recipes in the next chapter (for a real kick-start, scroll back to page 99 to get a feel for what a week menu in the ideal world can look like).

What to apply in the perceptible world (a.k.a. reality) regarding the Nutrient Hunter Compass:

1 Congratulations, you are now the CEO of your lifestyle! So you, and no one else, set the goals.

2 If you hit all your goals, good job! But it's worth remembering on the other days that, one circle in the compass is better than none. Mentally preparing for the fact that setbacks occur, makes it easier to accept them. Instead of feeling guilty, be proactive by 1) coming up with a way to deal with setbacks and 2) seeing them as a natural part of life and that you are aiming for sustainable long-term change.

3 Telling others about your intentions generates momentum. It also inspires others to hop onboard! When we do things in a group rather than on our own, we gain motivation, drive and a sense of community. Research tells us that it helps to make new habits long lasting ones. With the Nutrient Hunter Compass in hand, gather friends, family and colleagues and start a team expedition.

Dear fellow nutrient hunters, we have now gone through the entire Nutrient Hunter Compass which means that in 26.5 seconds you will be turning the page to the last chapter. In the next chapter we won't be babbling as much since we'll be in the kitchen and the recipes speak for themselves. All of the recipes are tailor-made for nutrient hunters and keep both the planet and our bodies happy. You can find stews, desserts, kid-friendly pasta sauces, savory salads and much more. And of course all of these recipes are crafted to help you fill in as many circles as possible in the Nutrient Hunter Compass.

1
2
3
4
6

Chapter N°5

THE KITCHEN

We're finally ready to enter the Nutrient Hunter's World! Here you will find an array of delicious recipes. We've even calculated the carbon footprint of each one (see page 25). View these recipes as inspiration... don't like an ingredient? Allergic? Try replacing it with something that suits you better.

P.S. Our website has oodles of recipes so visit us online if you're hungry for more! Truth be told, you can find recipes everywhere online today, just keep a lookout for ways you can tweak new recipes to optimize them for your new nutrient hunter lifestyle.

We said we wouldn't babble much in this chapter, so without further ado, grab your knives and get started!

MONDE
diplomatiq
l'ont tant aimé
Par Mathias Reymond
SOMMAIRE
www.monde-diplomatique.fr
FT Weekend

CARTE DES LIEUX DE POUVOIR À PARIS - Affiche en cahier central
LE MONDE diplomatique
LE PRESIDENT DES ULTRARICHES
PAR MICHEL PINÇON ET MONIQUE PINÇON-CHARLOT
Page 7.
5,40 € - Mensuel - 28 pages
QUELLES PRIORITÉS POUR JEREMY CORBYN?
Brexit de gauche, une voie étroite
PAR CHRIS BICKERTON
RECOMPOSITION POLITIQUE ET SOCIALE
Lutte de classes en France
PAR SERGE HALIMI ET PIERRE RIMBERT
CONFISCATION DE TERRES AU VIETNAM
Résistances paysannes
Assoiffé de croissance, le Vietnam mise sur l'essor des industries utilisatrices de main-d'œuvre et sur le développement de l'immobilier – sans regarder de trop près les conséquences pour l'environnement et pour les terres agricoles. Ce qui suscite la colère de nombreux paysans.
PAR NOTRE ENVOYÉ SPÉCIAL PIERRE DAUM
Février 2019
SOMMAIRE COMPLET EN PAGE 28
DÉSORMAIS EN POCHE
THOMAS PIKETTY
LE CAPITAL au XXIe siècle
2,5 MILLIONS D'EXEMPLAIRES VENDUS
UN SUCCÈS PLANÉTAIRE
"Piketty a transformé notre discours économique. Nous ne porlerons plus jamais de richesse et d'inégalité de la même manière."
Paul Krugman
POINTS HISTOIRE
Weekend
The New York Times

WEEKEND BRUNCH WITH PLATO

Some weekend mornings we jump into our robes and treat ourselves to a long breakfast with our favorite Plato.

2 baking sheets

GRANOLA WITH GINGER AND BANANA

- 2 cups Old Fashioned Oats (or steel cut)
- ½ cup sunflower seeds
- ½ cup pumpkin seeds
- ⅓ cup flaxseeds
- ⅓ cup chopped mixed nuts (or seeds if you're allergic)
- 2 Tbsp canola oil
- 1 Tbsp ground cinnamon
- 2 tsp ground ginger
- 1 tsp salt
- 2 green bananas

Granola with a twist - a green banana - that gives 1) sweetness and 2) big, crunchy pieces. Totally addictive!

Soak the oats overnight. Preheat the oven to 100°C/200°F if using convection (or 125°C/250°F in a regular oven, in which case, it's also best to bake one sheet at a time).

Drain the oats well and combine all the dry ingredients in a large bowl. Mash the bananas with a fork in another bowl, then combine with the oil. Stir the bananas into the dry ingredients and mix until everything is combined.

Spread the granola into a thin layer on two baking sheets (note: use two sheets even though it may feel like everything fits onto one, this way you'll get a really crunchy granola) and bake in the middle of the oven for about 3 hours, stirring every now and then and breaking apart overly large chunks until everything is crispy.

1,1

Two sheets (the entire recipe) emits 1,09 kg CO_2e

6 sandwiches

SWEET POTATO SANDWICH

1 Sweet potato

Topping Ideas

Nut butter, apple and sprouts

Red beet hummus (page 141), spinach, and seeds

Pea pesto (page 161), sunflower sprouts, and pickled carrot

Sweet potato as a sandwich? Absolutely. Serve for breakfast, as a snack, or as finger food at a mingle party.

Scrub the potatoes well, then cut into ½ inch thick slices lengthwise. Steam the slices for approximately 5 minutes until the pieces have softened. Garnish with preferred toppings.

QUICK TIP!

The perfect mingle food. Cut the potatoes widthwise instead, into round slices, and steam or bake in the oven brushed with a little oil. Allow to cool and then top with different garnishes to serve as finger food.

1 cup

TURMERIC LATTE

- ½ + ½ cup preferred plant-based milk
- 1 Tbsp light tahini
- ¼ tsp ground turmeric
- ⅛ tsp ground cinnamon
- 1 pinch of ground ginger
- 1 pinch of ground cloves
- 1 pinch of freshly ground black pepper

Inspired by the classic coffee drink, Food Pharmacy's golden milk gets a revamp. Invite friends over for breakfast and surprise them with one of these!

Heat ½ cup milk, tahini, and spices in a pot and whisk until smooth and foamy. Heat up the other ½ cup of milk and froth it with an immersion blender.

Pour the hot drink into a large mug, top with foamed milk, and dust with a little extra cinnamon.

QUICK TIP!

Be sure to choose milk that can be frothed, it usually says on the package.

<0,1

One cup emits 0,09 kg CO_2e

2 portions per sort

BREAKFAST ICE CREAM x 3

The one minute breakfast. (Don't worry, we won't tell anyone you eat ice cream for breakfast. P.S. These are delicious anytime - morning, day, or night.)

BERRY ICE CREAM (WITH A SECRET INGREDIENT)

150g/1 cup mixed berries, such as strawberries, lingon berries, blackberries or blue berries
150g/1 cup frozen cauliflower
½ cup plant-based milk
1 Tbsp light tahini
1 Tbsp fresh ginger

Thaw the cauliflower for 5 minutes (just so it's not rock hard). Grate the ginger and place all ingredients into a blender. Mix until smooth.

0,1

One portion emits 0,13 kg CO_2e

LINGON ICE CREAM

2 frozen green bananas
1 cup frozen lingonberries
½ cup plant-based milk
2 fresh dates, pitted

Toss everything in the blender and mix until smooth.

0,1

One portion emits 0,12 kg CO_2e

CHOCOLATE ICE CREAM

2 frozen green bananas
2 Tbsp cacao, raw
1 Tbsp unsweetened peanut butter
1 Tbsp cacao nibs
1 pinch of salt

Toss everything in the blender and mix until smooth.

QUICK TIP!

For a sweeter taste you can use ripe bananas. They provide less fiber and more sugar, but it's better than other alternatives.

0,1

One portion emits 0,09 kg CO_2e

FOOD

BAKING WITH GREEN SECRETS

As a nutrient hunter, we take every opportunity we get to hide vegetables and legumes in our pastries.

2 baking sheets

OAT CRISPBREAD WITH RED LENTILS

½ cup dried red lentils, soaked for at least 10 hours
¾ cup rolled oats
1 cup pumpkin seeds
¼ cup flax seeds
1 ½ Tbsp chia seeds
1 ½ Tbsp psyllium husk
½ tsp sea salt + extra to sprinkle
1 cup of boiling water
2 Tbsp cold pressed canola oil

This recipe is more than just a crispbread, it works as chips with dip (like the ones on pages 160–161) or an open face sandwich with breakfast toppings.

Drain and rinse the lentils. Combine the dry ingredients and lentils in a bowl. Add the boiling water and oil, mix everything until combined. Allow to rest for 10 minutes.

Roll half of the dough out thin between two parchment sheets, repeat with the other half. Place on two baking sheets, remove the top paper and sprinkle with salt. Press the salt to help it stick. Let the dough rest for 30 minutes.

Preheat oven to 150°C/300°F. Bake one at a time in the center of the oven for 60 minutes, remove and give the pan a turn, then bake for 10-20 minutes more or until completely dry and crispy. Allow to cool on the pan.

QUICK TIP!

If you have a convection oven you can lower the temperature to 125°C/275°F on the hot air function and bake both sheets at the same time.

0,6

2 sheets (the whole recipe) emits 0,6 kg CO_2e

10 small scones

SCONES (WITH BUTTER BEANS)

1 can (about 230g drained) butter beans
¼ cup light tahini
¼ cup water
1 cup oat flour
½ cup rolled oats
2 tsp baking powder
2 tsp ground cinnamon
½ tsp salt
1 ½ cup (150g) grated parsnip (or carrot)
¼ cup of hemp seeds (husked), sesame seeds or nuts

Moist scones with butter beans as the secret ingredient - a great way to get extra fiber.

Preheat oven to 120°C/250°F. Drain and rinse the beans. Blend the beans, tahini and water until smooth in a blender. Mix all dry ingredients in a bowl. Finely grate the parsnip and combine everything together into a batter.

Spoon ten dollops of dough on a lined baking sheet. Bake in the middle of the oven for 60-70 minutes, until the scones have a nice crust. Serve with chia berry jam for a sweet treat, or hummus and apple slices for a more savory snack. Or just eat them as they are.

<0,1

A portion of 2 scones emits 0,07 kg CO_2e

1 loaf

SEED LOAF (WITH YELLOW PEAS)

½ cup dried yellow peas (soaked for 12 hours)
2 medium carrots
½ cup walnuts
1 cup pumpkin seeds
½ cup hemp seeds
½ cup flax seeds
1 ½ cup oatmeal
¼ cup chia seeds
¼ cup psyllium husk
2 tsp salt
1 ½ cup boiling water
¼ cup cold pressed canola oil

Double the batch and make two loaves, cut into slices and store in the freezer - a perfect breakfast or snack for nutrient hunters.

Drain and rinse the peas then pulse them in a food processor into a crumble. Finely grate the carrots and roughly chop the walnuts. Combine all the dry ingredients and peas in a bowl. Pour the water and oil into the dry mixture and stir until well combined. Line bread loaf with parchment paper. Put the dough into the pan and press firmly so that you get a firm loaf. Let the dough take a siesta on the kitchen counter at room temperature for at least 2 hours.

Preheat oven to 150°C/300°F. Bake the bread in the middle of the oven for about 2 hours. Tip the bread out of the form and place it back in the oven on the rack. Bake for another 30 minutes, until the bread has a crust. Allow the bread to cool completely before slicing.

1,0

One loaf emits 0,97 kg CO_2e

2 sheets

GOLDEN GRANOLA WITH LENTILS, BUCKWHEAT AND APPLE

Base
1 cup dried red lentils
½ cup dried whole buckwheat
1 cup sunflower seeds
¼ cup chia seeds
1 cup mixed nuts, chopped
1 tsp salt
3 tsp ground cinnamon
2 tsp ground turmeric
2 tsp ground cardamom
¼ tsp ground cloves
¼ cup unsweetened applesauce

Add-ins
1 cup coconut flakes
2 cups of dried berries or fruit, e.g. mulberries, inca berries or apple

In this granola we've added red lentils to give the world's best crispiness (and a fiber bonus for the enthusiastic nutrient hunters). It is flavored with warm spices and sweetened with applesauce.

Soak the buckwheat and lentils separately overnight. Nighty Nighty!

Next day! Set the oven to 120°C/250°F. Rinse and drain the lentils and the buckwheat then pour onto a towel to dry slightly. Combine the rest of the ingredients and stir well to cover everything.

Pour out onto two lined baking sheets and spread out. Bake in the oven for 75-90 minutes, making sure to stir every now and then, until the granola is completely dry and deliciously crispy. Let cool. Add the coconut and dried berries to your granola and keep in a lidded container

1,0

2 sheets (the whole recipe) emits 1,04 kg CO_2e

PORRIDGE TWO WAYS

We nutrient hunters love porridge because it is an easy way to collect a lot of circles for different seeds, spices and grains in the Nutrient Hunter Compass at one and the same time. But also because it is so darn tasty!

1 serving

GOLDEN OVERNIGHT SEED PORRIDGE

Porridge
2 Tbsp rolled oats (soaked overnight or 8 hours)
¾ cup oat milk
4 Tbsp seed mixture (see recipe below)
¼ tsp ground turmeric
¼ tsp ground cinnamon
a pinch of salt
a pinch of fresh ground black pepper

Seed mix (yields 6 servings)
½ cup sunflower seeds
½ cup pumpkin seeds
½ cup hemp seeds
¼ cup flax seeds
¼ cup chia seeds

Apple and lingonberry compote (yields 6 servings)
2 red apples, diced
½ cup (100g) frozen lingonberries
½ tsp ground ginger
2 Tbsp water
1 pinch of salt

For those days when you want quick nutrition with a bit of a bite. Mix up a large batch of your seed mix ahead of time - a good way to take the shortcut in the morning, something we never turn down.

Stir the seed mixture together.

Drain the oats. Heat all porridge ingredients in a pot over medium heat until the porridge has thickened.

Toss all of the compote ingredients into a separate pot and simmer until softened. Top your porridge with the compote and sprinkle with some seeds.

QUICK TIP!

Soak a large batch of oats all at once, just use what you need and store the rest in the fridge. Perfect for making porridge, adding to soups or baking. Holds for at least three days.

Also!

Replace the ground ginger in the compote with cinnamon or cardamom for small kiddos who find ginger too spicy.

0,1

1 serving emits 0,14 kg CO_2e

2 servings

UNIVERSAL PORRIDGE WITH BUCKWHEAT AND BEANS

Porridge

¾ cup whole buckwheat (soaked overnight)
½ cup oatmeal
2 medium carrots
1 tsp ground turmeric
½ tsp ground ginger
2 ½ cup oat milk
A pinch of salt

Topping

½ cup kale
¾ cup (100g) pre-cooked butter beans
1 Tbsp light tahini
1 Tbsp water
A pinch of salt
2 Tbsp hemp seeds

With spices and savory ingredients you can easily transform a porridge into a meal fit for any time of day.

Remove the stem of the kale and tear the leaves into smaller pieces. Steam for 2 minutes. Strain and rinse the beans. Mix together tahini, water and a pinch of salt. Mix with the beans.

Drain and rinse the buckwheat. Finely grate the carrots. Cook the buckwheat, carrots and oatmeal with the oat milk in a pot for 7-10 minutes until thickened. Add the spices and season with salt.

Serve the porridge topped with steamed kale, beans and hemp seeds.

VARIATION!

- **Replace the buckwheat with steel cut oats.**
- **Switch out the carrot for something else -zucchini parsnip and pumpkin are our favorites.**
- **Replace the kale with some other leafy green.**
- **Replace the beans with another legume - chickpeas, kidney beans and beluga lentils are extra nom!**

QUICK TIP!

Save the stem from the kale, cut into pieces and save for the next time you make kale soup. Kale stems freeze well.
And!
If you add 2 teaspoons of apple cider vinegar per 3 cups of water when soaking grains, you help the soaking process to be more effective.

0,2

1 serving with toppings emits 0,18 kg CO_2e

LUNCH AND
DINNER

4 servings per sort

CLIMATE SMART EXOTIC DISHES

We love the ramen, palak paneer and poké bowls, but as environmentally conscious nutrient hunters we have realized the need for other variations of these dishes to reduce the carbon footprint many of them acquire as the ingredients travel across our seas.

RAMEN WITH VEGGIES, SPROUTS AND SAUERKRAUT

Ramen
4 inches/10 cm of a leek
1 garlic clove
1 head of broccoli
2 cups/200g oyster mushrooms
3 medium carrots
2 packages (300g) of kelp noodles or glass noodles
1 cup sauerkraut
A handful (50g) sprouts or pea shoots

Broth
2 Tbsp dark miso paste
4 Tbsp light tahini
3 ½ cups water

Garnish
2 handfuls fresh herbs, such as coriander, Thai basil or parsley

Ramen is a Japanese dish with noodles and vegetables served in broth. This variety is plant-based and made with veggies that are often cultivated in western countries.

Divide the leeks in the middle and rinse, cut into thin slices. Finely chop the garlic. Bring the water for the broth to a boil and stir in the miso and tahini. Add the leeks and garlic. Simmer on low heat while preparing the rest.

Break broccoli into smaller bouquets. Tear the mushroom into strips. Julienne the carrots. Strain the noodles and toss into the broth, simmer for max 5 minutes. Remove from the heat and toss in the carrots.

Steam broccoli for 5 minutes and blanch in cold water to retain crispiness. Fry the mushrooms in a frying pan with a splash of water until softened and slightly golden.

Divide the soup into 4 bowls. Add broccoli, mushrooms, sauerkraut and sprouts. Garnish with fresh herbs.

QUICK TIP!

You can also skip the noodles completely and increase the amount of veggies, finely shredded cabbage would be a nice addition!

0,3

1 serving emits 0,35 kg CO_2e

PLANET FRIENDLY POKÉ BOWL

Bowl

1 cup oat groats, uncooked (soak overnight or 8 hours)
½ (300g) celeriac bulb
1 cup (100g) chopped kale
1 cup (100g) red cabbage
Handful (50g) sprouts (e.g., lentil, bean or beetroot sprouts)
fresh parsley

Pickled carrots

2 medium carrots
¼ cup apple cider vinegar

Beet filling

1 red beet
1 can (230g) cooked white beans
sea salt

Horseradish sauce

1 cup plant-based yoghurt
1 tsp finely grated fresh horseradish
sea salt and freshly ground black pepper

Poké bowls come from Hawaii, but in this version we've switched out the white rice for more nutritious whole oats and used vegetables in place of the fish.

Prepare the oats according to the instructions. Scrub the celeriac and cut into thin slices. Steam for 5-7 minutes, until the celeriac is soft. Toss in the kale at the last minute to lightly steam it as well. Finely slice the cabbage.

Scrub and grate the carrots. Put in a bowl and pour over the vinegar. Let stand for at least 15 minutes.

Scrub and grate the beet. Mix together the rest of the beet filling ingredients and season with salt. Combine all of the Horseradish sauce ingredients in a separate bowl. Divide the oats amongst the bowls and top with all of the other ingredients, ending with the horseradish sauce. Garnish with parsley.

VARIATION!

Replace the carrot with fennel when in season.
Replace oats with other whole grains, such as barley or quinoa.
No parsley? Try some other herbs! Or switch it up with other cabbage sorts.

QUICK TIP!

Try adding any of the following proteins to your soup or bowl:

- **1 package (250g) of organic natural solid tofu - squeeze out the liquid, cut into cubes, marinate in tamari sauce 10 minutes and bake in the oven for 20 minutes.**
- **1 package tempeh (400g) - cut into thin slices and marinate in tamari sauce for 30 minutes. Put in a baking dish and bake for about 20 minutes at 150°C/300°F.**
- **1 package (230g) butter beans or chickpeas.**

0,1

1 serving emits 0,17 kg CO_2e

CLIMATE SMART PALAK PANEER

Palak paneer
1 yellow onion
2 garlic cloves
1 Tbsp fresh ginger
coconut oil for frying
2 ½ cups (400g) frozen whole spinach, thawed
2 packages (250g) of tofu, diced
1 package (500g) crushed tomatoes
1-2 tsp garam masala
1 tsp ground cumin
1 tsp ground turmeric
salt and freshly ground black pepper

Serve with
2 cups sorghum, or oat groats and fresh coriander

Palak paneer comes from India, but in this variation we have substituted the cream for crushed tomatoes and the cheese for tofu. Of course we kept all of the traditional spices that are often found in a classic palak paneer, gotta get those antioxidants!

Slice the onion and crush the garlic. Grate the ginger. Saute the onion and ginger together with some coconut oil in a large frying pan (cast iron is great!) until softened. Add the spinach and crushed tomatoes, simmer on low heat for 10 minutes. Toss in the tofu for the last few minutes as well as the spices so as not to destroy all the antioxidants. Season with salt.

Serve with cooked sorghum or oatmeal. Top with fresh coriander.

VARIATION!

Replace spinach with frozen kale.

0,3

1 serving emits 0,32 kg CO_2e

4 servings per sort

STEWS x 3

We love stews! Enough said.

VEGAN QUINOA CHILI

Chili

1 red onion
2 garlic cloves
coconut oil for frying
½ Tbsp ground cumin
½ tsp cayenne pepper
1 tsp smoked paprika powder
2 ½ cups water
2 cans crushed tomatoes
1 cup beluga lentils
1 cup red quinoa
1 can (230g) cooked kidney beans
3 medium carrots
1 Tbsp dried oregano
1 Tbsp olive oil
sea salt and freshly ground black pepper

Till servering

leafy greens (like spinach and kale)
plant-based yogurt

A savory and filling stew due to the combination of legumes, quinoa and carrots, perfect for nutrient hunters!

Dice the onions and chop the garlic. Saute until soft in a little oil along with the spices. Add the water, crushed tomatoes, lentils and quinoa. Simmer on low heat for about 15 minutes, until the lentils and quinoa are cooked through.

Rinse and drain the kidney beans. Grate the carrots and toss into the chili with the oregano. Add a little more water if needed. Season with salt and pepper.

Remove the pot from the heat and leave the chili to rest with the lid on for 20 mins before serving.

Serve with a handful of mixed leafy greens and a spoonful of yogurt.

0,1

1 serving emits 0,15 kg CO_2e

BAM

RED LENTIL AND ZUCCHINI BOWL

Base

1 cup red lentils
1 Tbsp light tahini
1 tsp apple cider vinegar
1 Tbsp ground turmeric
sea salt and freshly ground black pepper

Topping

1 cup sorghum, uncooked
1 zucchini
1 head of cauliflower
4 Tbsp pea pesto (see page 161, optional)
Handful (70g) of mixed leafy greens
¼ cup roasted sunflower seeds
sea salt and freshly ground black pepper

Somewhere between a stew and a casserole, this dish gets served up in a bowl with an herby topping. Feel free to switch up the veggies for more seasonal picks throughout the year.

Cook the lentils as instructed on the package. Strain and combine with all of the ingredients for the base (add a splash of water if too dry). Season with salt and pepper.

Cook the sorghum according to the instructions on the package. Cut the zucchini into crescents, break the cauliflower into smaller bouquets. Steam the zucchini and cauliflower for 5–7 minutes, until they are slightly softened, but crisp in the center. Allow to cool slightly, then mix together with the pea pesto and sorghum.

Divide the base into 4 bowls. Top with a handful of salad, and pesto mixture. Sprinkle with sunflower seeds.

QUICK TIP!

Have a bunch of leftovers in the fridge? Make the red lentil base and top with whatever you have at home.
And!
Feel free to sprout the lentils before cooking them to get even more nutrition from them.

0,2

One portion emits 0,19 kg CO_2e

GUT FRIENDLY CURRY STEW WITH GARLIC AND CORIANDER

Stew
1-2 Tbsp curry seasoning (p. 169)
2 Tbsp cold pressed canola oil
1 yellow onion
2 garlic cloves
⅓ cup apricots
1 ¼ cup dried red or yellow lentils
1 can crushed tomatoes
1 ½ cup water

Celery and apple salsa
2 stalks of celery
2 red apples
1 handful fresh herbs, e.g., parsley/mint/basil
2 Tbsp apple cider vinegar
sea salt and freshly ground black pepper

Serve with
4 servings of whole grains, for example sorghum/oat groats/quinoa
fresh coriander

Warming, satiating and delicious - it also saves great as leftovers or to pack as lunch for the next day. Heat the dried spices over low heat with a bit of oil in a saucepan until they become fragrant.

Chop the onions and garlic, toss in a pot with the spices and some oil and saute until softened. Finely chop the apricots. Pour the lentils, apricots, crushed tomatoes and water into the pot and simmer on low heat for about 30 minutes, stirring every now and then until you have a creamy lentil stew.

If you think the stew is too thick, add some extra water. When the lentils are cooked through, remove the pot from the heat and allow it to stand for a while with the lid on to let the flavors marinate a bit.

Salsa: Grate the apples. Cut the celery into thin slices. Chop the herbs. Mix together the ingredients for the salsa. Season with salt and pepper.

QUICK TIP!

This dish is perfect for making a large batch since it only gets better the day after.

VARIATION!

Try one of these combinations:

- **Grated parsnip, grated carrot, parsley**
- **Fine sliced kale, cooked chickpeas, coriander**
- **Fresh tomatoes, white beans and spinach**
- **Green beans, broccoli and coriander**

0,2

1 serving emits 0,24 kg CO_2e

4 servings

FOOD PHARMACY'S GOLDEN SOUP

Soup

2 Tbsp cold pressed canola oil
½ yellow onions
1 garlic clove
1 head of cauliflower head
4 medium carrots
½ cup of raw cashews
(soaked for 2–4 hours)
2 tsp ground turmeric
5 cups of water
1 Tbsp apple cider vinegar
1 tsp herb blend (see page 168)
sea salt and freshly ground
black pepper

Topping

1 can (230g) of cooked
chickpeas
½ tsp cold pressed canola oil
½ tsp herb mix (see p. 168)
cauliflower leaves or (1 cup kale)

Cauliflower, carrots and cashews together with warming spices make this soup a golden favorite. And remember - Use all parts of the plant, which in this case means using up the cauliflower leaves as a topping!

Preheat oven to 100°C/200°F. Drain, rinse and dry the chickpeas, dry with paper towels. Roast on a baking sheet in the middle of the oven for 20 minutes.

Drain and rinse the cashews.

Preheat oven to 175°C/350°F. Remove the outer leaves of the cauliflower, save them. Brush the leaves with 1 teaspoon oil and a pinch of salt. Place on a baking sheet and roast in the center of the oven for about 10 minutes (may need to be flipped half way).

Chop the onion and garlic, saute until soft in a little coconut oil in a pot. Divide the cauliflower into smaller pieces, slice the carrots. Place cauliflower and carrots in the pot along with the nuts, water and turmeric. Simmer until the cauliflower has softened. Mix until completely smooth with an immersion blender, or pour into a blender and blend until you have a smooth and creamy soup. Season with vinegar, salt and pepper, dilute with more water if you desire a thinner soup. Finally, add the herbs and pulse a few times more with the mixer.

Serve the soup with the roasted chickpeas and cauliflower leaves.

VARIATION!

Try serving with roasted white beans or sprouted lentils instead of chickpeas. The parsley can be replaced with any herb, and the cauliflower leaves could be replaced with savoy cabbage.

0,2

One portion emits 0,14 kg CO_2e

THREE QUICK PASTA SAUCES

In ten minutes tops you can assemble a vibrant and delicious nutrient hunter style sauces using vegetables as the base. Start by serving over your regular pasta, or try spiralized veggie noodles if you're in the mood. There's no time to lose - ready, set, sauce time!

About 1 1/2 cups

GREEN KALE SAUCE WITH GARLIC AND PARSLEY

1 cup (125g) of frozen kale
1 garlic clove
½ cup walnuts
½ cup plant-based milk
1 Tbsp nutritional yeast
1 Tbsp apple cider vinegar
1 Tbsp parsley (fresh/frozen)
sea salt and freshly ground black pepper

This green sauce comes together in the blink of an eye.

Thaw the kale. Crush the garlic. Toss everything in a blender and mix until smooth! Season with salt and pepper. Pour into a saucepan and warm the sauce.

0,2

1 ½ cups sauce emits 0,21 kg CO_2e

About 1 1/2 cups

HERBY HUMMUS SAUCE

1 can (230g) of cooked chickpeas
2 handfuls mixed fresh herbs, try basil and parsley
1 garlic clove
½ cup water
1 Tbsp apple cider vinegar
sea salt and freshly ground black pepper

Hummus. This fantastic spread that's good on a slice of seed bread, a crunchy crispbread or as salad condiment - turned into a sauce!

Drain and rinse the chickpeas. Mix all of the ingredients together in a blender until smooth. Season with salt and pepper. Add a splash of water for a thinner sauce. Warm if desired.

<0,1

1 ½ cups sauce emits 0,06 kg CO_2e

About 1 1/2 cups

RED PEPPER SAUCE

2 red bell peppers
1 cup (100g) cremini mushrooms
1 red onion
1 garlic clove
1 tsp of parsley (dried/fresh/ frozen)
2 Tbsp nutritional yeast
1 Tbsp apple cider vinegar
¼ - ½ cup plant-based milk
sea salt and freshly ground black pepper

We love everything about this sauce. A top notch recipe for nutrient hunters!

Dice the peppers, chop the mushrooms and dice the red onion. Crush the garlic. Steam peppers, mushrooms and onions for 10 minutes, until soft. Pour into a blender and mix with the rest of the ingredients into a smooth sauce. Season with salt and pepper.

ROOKIE STYLE FOR YOU

When making zoodles (zucchini noodles), it is always wise to let them soak in cold water for 10 minutes. That way they become crispy and reach the next level of good.

1,1

1 ½ cups sauce emits 1,09 kg CO_2e

FLATBREAD THREE WAYS

This flatbread is made from two ingredients, boiled potato and chick-pea flour, and it is a-m-a-z-i-n-g. Eat it just as it is or try one of the variations below. Climate impact varies depending on how you top your bread.

8 flatbreads

BASIC FLATBREAD RECIPE

4 medium waxy potatoes, boiled
¾ - 1 cup chickpea flour (depending on how wet the potatoes are)
½ tsp fine sea salt

Allow the potatoes to cool after they've been boiled. Finely grate the potatoes. Knead the grated potatoes with the chickpea flour and salt into a dough. Divide the dough into 8 balls. Roll each one out on a floured countertop.

Fry in a dry pan over medium heat until the bread begins to have some color, flip over and fry on the other side. Repeat for all 8 pieces. Store wrapped in a clean kitchen towel until serving so they don't dry out.

VARIATION!

Replace chickpea flour with buckwheat or durum flour. Or add 1 tsp fennel seeds (crushed).

0,2

The whole batch emits 0,15 kg CO_2e

SANDWICH

1 batch of potato flatbread - see recipe above

Sandwich filling ideas
Yellow pea hummus, shredded apple, beet sprouts
Green pea spread, sliced bell pepper, pea shoots
Sweet potato slices*, massaged kale, no oil aioli
Sweet potato slices*, cucumber, tomato

Serve freshly baked bread for weekend breakfast, topped with spreads, crispy vegetables and sprouts. You can also cut into smaller slices and serve as finger food?

* Scrub 1 sweet potato. Cut into super thin slices, brush with olive oil and bake in the oven at 120°C/250°F until tender. Use as toppings.

4 servings

PIZZA YOUR WAY

Simple tomato sauce
1 garlic clove
¾ cup tomato puree
¼ cup water
1 tsp dried oregano
1 tsp apple cider vinegar
salt and freshly ground black pepper

Topping ideas
Mushrooms, tomatoes, peppers, arugula, pea pesto (page 161), zucchini, pine nuts, thinly sliced squash, thinly sliced onion

Here we use our flatbread and top it with lots of different things. Fun tip, especially for little ones, is to prepare different bowls with different toppings and let everyone top their own pizza.

Bake the bread as instructed on the left. Crush the garlic and mix the ingredients for the tomato sauce together in a bowl. Spread a bit of sauce on a ready-made flatbread and top with preferred veggies. Bake the pizzas at 150°C/300°F until the toppings have cooked and are slightly golden, about 30 minutes.

VARIOUS WRAPS

For adults (or kids)
1 packet of smoked tofu
100 g kale

Red beet hummus
1 can (230g) cooked chickpeas
2 garlic cloves
3 cooked beets
4 Tbsp olive oil
1 Tbsp light tahini
1 tsp ground cumin
sea salt and freshly ground black pepper
1 lemon, juiced

For kids (or adults)
1 pack of smoked tofu
simple tomato sauce (see recipe above)
spinach

Few dishes are as brilliant as wrap: a bread filled with whatever your heart desires that you can eat with your hands at home or on the go.

Make the flatbread as instructed to the left.

Mix everything for the beet hummus in a blender. Season with salt, pepper and lemon juice.

Cut tofu into slices, fry gently on medium heat with a little oil until the pieces are warm. Put some beet hummus or tomato sauce on the bread. Remove the stem from the kale, tear the leaves into smaller pieces. Steam for 2 minutes. Fill the wrap with tofu and your chosen greens.

4 servings

WOK WITH BRUSSEL SPROUTS, MUSHROOMS AND SUNCHOKES

Wok

½ cup sorghum
5 cups (500g) brussel sprouts
3 cups (300g) of mushrooms, e.g. chanterelles or cremini
2 cups (250g) sunchokes
3 Tbsp olive oil
2 tsp sea salt
½ tsp freshly ground black pepper
Handful of fresh parsley

Green pea hummus

3 cups (500g) frozen green peas (thawed)
1 cup (100g) spinach
1 package of fresh coriander
1 garlic clove
2 Tbsp light tahini
1 Tbsp apple cider vinegar

This wok is something extraordinary. With brussel sprouts, mushrooms and sunchokes it collects a stunning amount of circles in the Nutrient Hunter Compass.

Cook the sorghum as directed on the package. Mix the ingredients for the pea hummus in a food processor. Season with salt and pepper.

Clean the brussel sprouts and split them in half. Slice the mushrooms in half. Peel the sunchokes and slice them thinly, a mandolin works great for this.

Heat a little oil in a frying pan and fry the brussel sprouts for about 5 minutes. Add the mushrooms and sunchokes and fry while stirring until everything has a bit of color, about 5 minutes. Add the sorghum and season with salt and pepper. Serve with the green pea hummus. Garnish with parsley.

0,4

1 serving emits 0,38 kg CO_2e

4 servings

FOOD PHARMACY'S WEEKDAY FAVORITES

Hello stroganoff, meatballs and all-in-one dishes - we took the liberty of adapting you to suit a nutrient hunter's lifestyle.

FOOD PHARMACY'S STROGANOFF

Stroganoff
1 yellow onion
1 garlic clove
coconut oil for frying
1 can crushed tomatoes
3 Tbsp tomato puree
1 Tbsp dijon mustard
1 cup plant-based cream
2 ½ cups (250g) cremini mushrooms, or other preferred mushroom
400g tempeh
salt and freshly ground black pepper

Serve with
Cooked grains and mixed leafy greens

A classic with a Food Pharmacy twist. We used pieces of tempeh - a fermented product made from soybeans. Serve with your favorite grain (or pseudocereal) - sorghum, oat groats, buckwheat or quinoa for example.

Mince the onion and garlic, saute in a pan with coconut oil until softened. Add crushed tomatoes, tomato puree, mustard and milk. Let simmer for 5 minutes. Slice the mushrooms. Add to the pan and cook for another 5 minutes.

Cut the tempeh into pieces. Fy in a pan over medium heat with a little coconut oil, until they turn golden, then add them to the tomato mixture and let everything simmer for a few more minutes. Season with salt and pepper. Serve with a side, such as whole buckwheat or oat groats and mixed leafy greens.

QUICK TIP!

If you can't get tempeh, you can use tofu or butter beans. If you use tofu, it is best to squeeze out as much liquid as possible. Place tofu between two paper towels and squeeze with your hands.

0,4

One portion emits 0,43 kg CO_2e

MEATBALLS SANS MEAT

"Meatballs"
1 ¾ cup beluga lentils
1 ½ cup of red quinoa
1 yellow onion
3 garlic cloves
2 Tbsp canola oil + a little to fry
2 Tbsp fennel seeds
¾ cup of sunflower seeds
1 tsp chili powder
2 carrots
1 ¼ cups of sun-dried tomatoes
3 Tbsp white wine vinegar
1 Tbsp dijon mustard
2 Tbsp of potato starch
1 Tbsp finely chopped parsley
2 Tbsp buckwheat flour

Simple tomato sauce
1 red onion
1 garlic
1 can crushed tomatoes
1 handful of fresh basil or 2 Tbsp frozen
1 handful of fresh parsley or 2 Tbsp frozen
1 Tbsp canola oil
sea salt and freshly ground black pepper

This recipe is one that we received from our friend Alena Grahn who is a chef at Rosendahl's Garden in Sweden. We only have two things to say: Yum and Thanks!

Boil the lentils in lightly salted water until they are al dente. Cook the quinoa according to the package plus a pinch of salt. Roast the fennel seeds in a pan until fragrant and grind them in a mortar once they have cooled.

Finely dice the onions and crush the garlic, saute with a bit of oil over low heat until softened. Add the ground fennel seeds and chili powder. Grate the carrots.

Pour the sunflower seeds into a food processor and mix them into a coarse ground texture. Add the rest of the ingredients and pulse until everything comes together. Taste the mixture and season with salt and pepper accordingly.

Roll into balls and fry with a bit of canola oil in a pan over low-medium heat.

Make the tomato sauce by frying the onion and garlic in canola oil until softened. Add the rest of the ingredients and let it simmer for 5 minutes. Season with salt and pepper.

Serve the tomato sauce with the "meatballs" and perhaps a grain such as buckwheat or oat groats on the side.

0,4

One portion emits 0,4 kg CO_2e

ALL-IN-ONE-PAN

Base
1 yellow onion
4 potatoes
4 carrots
2 parsnips
½ celeriac bulb
1 zucchini
1 handful of fresh basil
1 Tbsp cold pressed canola oil
sea salt and freshly ground black pepper

Mustard sauce
1 Tbsp unsweetened coarse mustard
2 Tbsp cold pressed olive oil
1 Tbsp water
1 Tbsp honey
1 Tbsp apple cider vinegar
sea salt and freshly ground black pepper

Serve with
spinach
hummus or other legumes (see pages 160–161)

All-in-one-pan dishes are some of the smartest dishes in the world. The basic idea is to cut different foods up and toss them together with a few seasoning and then prepare them all at the same time - oven baked, steamed or fried in cast iron skillet. Mostly, we just look at it as a good carrier for this mustard sauce.

Preheat oven to 120°C/250°F. Chop the onions and mince the garlic. Clean and dice the potatoes, carrots, parsnips, zucchini and celeriac into small even cubes. Put everything on a baking sheet and mix with oil, salt and pepper. Roast in the middle of the oven until everything is soft, but still has some cripisness (about 45 minutes).

Combine all the sauce ingredients in a bowl. Serve with a handful of spinach, basil and possibly another side such as hummus or legumes.

VARIATION!

Most vegetables work great for this dish - let the season and the contents of your fridge lead the way.

- **Spring - carrots, cabbage, red cabbage, peas and asparagus.**
- **Summer - green beans, zucchini, fresh onions, new potatoes, tomatoes**
- **Autumn - apple, kale, cauliflower, leeks, carrot, savoy cabbage**
- **Winter - root vegetables and cabbage of all kinds - beets, carrot, parsnip, celeriac, white cabbage, red cabbage, kale, brussel sprouts.**

ROOKIE STYLE FOR YOU

Try to combine at least three different colors of veggies.

0,1

One portion emits 0.11 kg CO_2e

4 servings

FOOD PHARMACY TACOS

Food Pharmacy's taco base

1 ½ cups (230g) cooked lentils
1-2 tsp tacos seasoning (page 168)

Taco toppings

lettuce leaves and/or taco shells,
crispy vegetables like cabbage, bell peppers, cucumber,
diced tomatoes mixed with fresh herbs like coriander and parsley,
roasted veggies
tzatsiki-ish (page 165)

Tacos have never come together so easily as this recipe. Season the lentils with taco seasoning to replace classic beef and add all your favorite toppings and sides. We usually go with crispy lettuce leaves in place of taco shells but the kids tend to stick with the corn tortillas. Remember - as a nutrient hunter there is no right or wrong!

Prepare all of the toppings and sides you plan to serve and put in small bowls. Drain and rinse the lentils. Heat in a pan on low heat along with the taco seasoning until everything is warm. Let everyone create their own individual tacos from the muy delicioso spread you've created!

QUICK TIP!

Add some finely chopped mushrooms, finely chopped eggplant, finely chopped white cabbage or some sunflower seeds (mixed to a coarse crumb) to the taco base if you want to boost it with even more nutrients.

<0,1

Entire taco base emits 0,06 kg CO_2e

4 servings

THERMOS SOUP

2 cups red quinoa, cooked
1 head of broccoli
½ head of cauliflower
1 cup (150g) of cremini mushrooms
2 carrots
1 zucchini
2 green onions
1 liter of vegetable broth
1 cup (150g) sugar snap peas (go with frozen if not in season)
1 handful of fresh spinach
1 handful coriander
salt and freshly ground black pepper

Thermos soup is really handy! Put raw vegetables and cooked grains into a jar and pour over steaming hot broth from a thermos just before serving! Perfect for a take-along anywhere meal. The veggies below are our suggestions, but of course you could vary the ingredients infinitely.

Break the broccoli and cauliflower into smaller bouquets, remember to cut the stem into thin slices. Slice the mushrooms and julienne the carrots and zucchini. Slice the green onions and use the whole stem!

Bring the broth to a simmer and fill up your thermos. Divide the quinoa into the bottom of four jars or bowls, place the vegetables on top. To serve just pour over the broth and allow the vegetables to steep for a few minutes in the warm broth.

ROOKIE STYLE FOR YOU

If you find the vegetables too crunchy, steam them for 3-5 minutes before you put them in the jar.

0,2

One portion emits 0,15 kg CO_2e

4 servings

ROASTED CAULIFLOWER WITH TAHINI, TURMERIC AND DUKKAH

Steaks
1 head of cauliflower
½ Tbsp cold-pressed canola oil

Tahini sauce with turmeric
¼ cup light tahini
4 Tbsp water
1 Tbsp apple cider vinegar
½ tsp ground turmeric
2 fresh dates
sea salt and freshly ground black pepper

Serve with
2 red apples
2 small (250g) roasted onions
1 package (250g) mixed tomatoes
1 handful of leafy greens
2 tsp dukkah (page 169)
cooked grains - oats groats, sorghum or wild rice

If you can't go to New York then New York will have to come to you. This dish is normally served on ABCV in Union Square, but we've recreated it in our homes with a few small nutrient hunter tweaks.

Preheat oven to 150°C/300°F. Break off any leaves from the cauliflower. Brush the whole cauliflower and leaves with oil. Slice the apples and onions into wedges.

Place the cauliflower in a baking dish, roast in the middle of the oven for 75–90 minutes (depending on how large the cauliflower is), toss the apples and onions in for the last 40 minutes or until the cauliflower is tender to the core and has a golden brown surface.

Mix together the ingredients for the dressing. Season with salt and pepper.

Place the cauliflower on a serving platter and serve with leafy greens, apples and onions around it. Drizzle the dressing over everything and sprinkle with dukkah, serve with grains.

0,2

One portion emits 0,23 kg CO_2e

4 servings

BAKED POTATOES WITH THE ULTIMATE TOPPER

4 sweet potatoes
1 small red onion
200g of natural tofu
½ lemon
½ package dill
¾ cup vegan mayonnaise (see recipe to the right under Quick Tip)
1 jar of seaweed caviar
sea salt and freshly ground black pepper

What ever happened to baked potatoes? We're taking it upon ourselves to give them a revival!

Preheat oven to 125°C/250°F. Prick the potatoes with a fork a few times. Place them on a lined baking sheet and bake them for 3 hours until soft. Remove from the oven and allow to cool slightly.

Chop the tofu into small pieces and zest the lemon. Mix everything together and season with salt, pepper, add a little lemon juice. Divide the sweet potatoes in the middle and add a dollop of topping on each half.

ROOKIE STYLE FOR YOU

This topping works well to serve in small salad leaves too, as an appetizer or a snack.

SCIENCE FOR YOU

We don't want to ruin the party, but we don't usually eat sweet potatoes every day because it increases blood sugar response and seems to reduce the feeling of satiation.

QUICK TIP!

Here's how to make vegan mayonnaise: Add 3 Tbsp chickpea cooking liquid (what you normally drain off), 1 tsp dijon mustard and 2 tsp freshly squeezed lemon juice into a blender and mix. Carefully drizzle 1-1 ¼ cup of canola oil while mixing until you get a thick and creamy mayonnaise.

0,3

One portion emits 0,29 kg CO_2e

4 servings

PAELLA WITH CAULIFLOWER RICE

1 head of cauliflower
1 yellow onion, diced
3 garlic cloves
coconut oil for frying
2 bell peppers, any color
10 small tomatoes
1 can (230g) cooked chickpeas
1 ½ cups frozen green peas, thawed
1 tsp saffron (5g)
1 cup white wine
½ cup vegetable broth
½ lemon, juiced
a handful of fresh parsley
sea salt and freshly ground black pepper

Yet another example of how easy it is to turn a classic recipe into a nutrient hunter meal that will fill lots of circles in the nutrient hunter compass.

Saute the onion in a pan with a bit of oil.

Chop the peppers, dice the tomatoes, rinse the chickpeas and toss all of them into the pan. Add the wine, broth and saffron, stir and simmer on low, until the cauliflower feels tender but not mushy. Add the peas towards the end. Season with salt and pepper and remove from heat. Garnish with a squeeze of the lemon, chopped fresh parsley and extra black pepper.

0,4

One portion emits 0,42 kg CO_2e

1 bowl of each

FOOD PHARMACY'S FIVE SAUCY SIDES

Dips, toppings and hummus - whatever you call them, they are a great way to increase the number of nutrients in any meal. Good on a salad, on crisp bread or on a freshly baked flatbread (page 140).

INTERN LENTIL DIP

¾ cup green lentils, cooked
¾ cup cashews, soaked overnight
1 cup frozen green peas, thawed
½ cup parsley
2 garlic cloves
1 Tbsp lemon juice
2 Tbsp canola oil
1 tsp of ground coriander
sea salt and freshly ground black pepper

There are interns and then there are interns who invent magic lentil dips. We prefer the latter.

Mix all the ingredients in a blender until you have a dip consistency you like. Season with salt and pepper (add a splash of water in some cases).

0,5

The entire bowl emits 0,54 kg CO_2e

SAUERKRAUT HUMMUS WITH WALNUTS

½ cup walnuts, soaked 1–4 hours
1 can (230g) cooked white beans
1 Tbsp cold pressed canola oil
1 handful of fresh parsley, finely chopped
1 garlic clove, finely chopped
½ cup sauerkraut
sea salt and freshly ground black pepper

An exciting variation of one of our favorite dips - hummus. Filled with fermented cabbage which makes your gut flora and taste buds very happy. Yum!

Drain and rinse the walnuts and beans. Toss everything in a blender and mix until smooth. Add some water if desired and season with salt and pepper.

0,1

The entire bowl emits 0,13 kg CO_2e

CARROT HUMMUS WITH CHICKPEAS AND CUMIN

4 medium (250g) carrots
1 can (230g) cooked chickpeas
1 garlic clove, crushed
1 tsp mortared cumin seeds
1 Tbsp cold pressed canola oil
1 Tbsp apple cider vinegar
1 Tbsp light tahini
¼ cup water
sea salt and freshly ground black pepper

Another variation of hummus, it gets its lovely color from the carrots and warm spice from the cumin. One of our new favorites!

Wash the carrots and steam until completely soft, about 15 minutes. Allow to cool. Drain off and rinse the chickpeas. Add everything to a blender and mix until smooth. Season with salt and pepper.

0,1

The entire bowl emits 0,12 kg CO_2e

GREEN PEA PESTO

2 cups (250g) frozen green peas, thawed
1 handful of kale, chopped
1 cup mixed fresh herbs
1 garlic clove, crushed
¼ cup sunflower seeds
1 Tbsp nutritional yeast (optional)
2 Tbsp cold pressed canola oil
1 Tbsp apple cider vinegar
sea salt and freshly ground black pepper

A fun and new way to serve green peas. Try topping your pizza with a few spoonfuls of this!

Mix all of the ingredients together in a mixer until you have a thick pesto. Season with salt and pepper.

QUICK TIP!

Try adding a few chili flakes for more flavor.

0,2

The entire bowl emits 0,2 kg CO_2e

CREAMY PARSNIP DIP

7 medium (500g) parsnips
2 tsp dijon mustard
2 handfuls of fresh basil
2 tablespoons chopped chives
¾ cup water
sea salt and freshly ground black pepper

A tasty dip with a lot of flavor, we love to serve it on top of a salad.

Clean the parsnips and chop into a medium dice. Steam the parsnip until soft, it takes about 10 minutes. Allow to cool. Combine all the ingredients in a blender and mix until smooth. Season with salt and pepper.

<0,1

The entire bowl emits 0,08 kg CO_2e

SUDOKU
NYBÖRJARE
MICHIKO YAMATO
ARCTIC

FOOD PHARMACY'S TOP FIVE SURVIVAL DRESSINGS

Five dressings to always have close at hand. Double the recipes and keep them in the fridge - an easy way to stay ahead of lunches and dinners.

About 1 1/2 cups

GREEN TAHINI DRESSING

½ cup light tahini
½ cup water
1 garlic clove, crushed
2 Tbsp freshly squeezed lemon juice
2 handfuls of mixed herbs
sea salt and freshly ground black pepper

Tahini, a paste made from sesame seeds, is the perfect base in a creamy dressing and it fits to just about everything. Choose a light tahini made from unroasted sesame seeds.

Mix all ingredients into a smooth dressing with an immersion blender. Season with salt and pepper.

0,1

1 ½ cups dressing emits 0,13 kg CO_2e

About 1 1/2 cups

TOP NOTCH BBQ-DRESSING

1 ½ cups crushed tomatoes
1 garlic clove, crushed
2 dates, pitted
1 Tbsp coarse grain mustard
3 Tbsp apple cider vinegar
1 tsp smoked paprika powder
1 tsp onion powder
1 tsp dried coriander
sea salt and freshly ground black pepper

A smoky and delicious dressing with tomato as a base - perfect to summer grilling to use as a marinade.

Whisk everything together! Season with salt and black pepper.

0,3

1 ½ cup dressing emits 0,26 kg CO_2e

About 1 1/2 cups

MISO DRESSING

1 package fresh coriander
1 big handful of spinach
¼ cup of pine nuts
1 cup of water
¼ cup freshly squeezed lemon juice
3 Tbsp dark miso paste
sea salt and freshly ground black pepper

Miso is a paste made from fermented soybeans that has a lot of umami flavor. Good to drizzle over savory salads and roasted carrots.

Whisk until smooth! Season with salt and pepper.

<0,1

1 ½ cups dressing emits 0,1 kg CO_2e

About 3/4 cup

WALNUT MUSTARD AND ONION VINAIGRETTE

½ cup water
1 Tbsp cold pressed canola oil
2 Tbsp apple cider vinegar
½ cup walnuts, (soaked 3 hrs)
1 tsp fennel seeds
1 tsp coarse mustard
2 tsp dried onion powder
sea salt and freshly ground black pepper

A savory vinaigrette with nutty tones. Any salad only gets better with this on it!

Put everything in a blender and mix until smooth! Season with salt and pepper.

0,1

¾ cup dressing emits 0,11 kg CO_2e

About 1 1/2 cups

TZATZIK-ISH

1 handful of fresh spinach
10 fresh mint leaves
1 cup plant-based yogurt
1 garlic clove, crushed
sea salt and freshly ground black pepper

A tzatziki with some nutrient hunter tweaks.

Toss everything in a food processor and pulse a few times! Season with salt and pepper.

<0,1

1 ½ cups dressing emits 0,09 kg CO_2e

ÖRTMIX
DUKK
TACOMYS

DET MESTA
CURRY

About 1 cup of each

FOOD PHARMACY'S FIVE FAV SPICES MIXES

Ready to go spice mixes simplify cooking significantly since you don't have to deal with a lot of small steps in the middle of cooking. It's also a great way to collect a few extra circles in the compass. These are not climate-calculated because the serving is so small that it is considered negligible.

QUICK TIP!

Store the spices in an airtight glass jar so they last for a long time

TACO SEASONING

4 Tbsp ground cumin
2 Tbsp paprika
2 Tbsp garlic powder
2 Tbsp onion powder
2 tsp dried oregano
¼ tsp cayenne pepper
4 tsp sea salt
2 tsp coarsely ground black pepper

Who doesn't love tacos?! Consider this one a basic necessity to have on hand.

Combine everything together and store in a glass jar.

HERB MIX

4 Tbsp dried thyme
4 Tbsp dried oregano
2 Tbsp dried parsley
2 tsp dried sage
2 tsp of dried rosemary
1 tsp sea salt

A good herb mix is perfect to have at home to season roasted vegetables, stews, dips or even a little herbal oil.

Combine all the herbs and salt together.

CURRY SPICE

3 Tbsp ground cinnamon
3 Tbsp ground ginger
2 Tbsp ground cumin
2 Tbsp ground turmeric
2 tsp chili powder
1 tsp ground cloves
1 tsp sea salt
½ tsp coarse ground black pepper

Seriously a fav, we use it all the time, especially in lentil stews.

Combine all the ingredients together.

WORKS-ON-EVERYTHING-SPICE

3 Tbsp fennel seeds
2 1/2 Tbsp cumin seeds
2 1/2 Tbsp coriander seeds
2 Tbsp paprika powder
2 Tbsp onion powder
1 Tbsp sea salt

Sprinkle this on pretty much anything and you're good to go, try it in falafels or on top of hummus.

Roast the whole seeds in a dry frying pan on low heat until they become fragrant. Cool completely. Mortar or grind into ground spices and mix with the rest of the ingredients.

DUKKAH

½ cup hazelnuts, soaked 8 hrs
4 Tbsp sesame seeds
2 Tbsp coriander seeds
2 Tbsp dried parsley leaves
1 Tbsp cumin seeds
1 Tbsp sea salt

An Egyptian spice blend that works great sprinkled over salads.

Drain and rinse the nuts. Place on a baking sheet and roast at 50°C/100°F in the oven overnight, until the nuts are completely dry. Finely chop the nuts and mix with the rest of the spices.

SWEETS AND
DESSERTS

CHOCOLATE X 4

We are crazy about chocolate of all forms. In addition, raw cacao contains a lot of antioxidants - which is good news for nutrient hunters.

4 servings

SECRET CHOCOLATE MOUSSE

Mousse
1 can (230g) cooked black beans
4 Tbsp raw cacao
10 fresh dates, pitted
¾ cup coconut milk
1 Tbsp hazelnut butter
½ tsp apple cider vinegar
1 pinch of salt

Topping ideas
whipped coconut cream
cacao nibs
berries and in season fruits

Chocolate fluff at its best, it's also a lot more fun to serve sweets that contain fiber and nutrients!

Mix all the ingredients for the mousse in a blender for a fairly long time until you get a completely smooth mousse. Place in 4 bowls and add toppings.

QUICK TIP!

Add 1 tablespoon of strong coffee for a more adult touch.

0,3

One portion emits 0.25 0,25 kg CO_2e

2 glasses

CHOCOLATE MILKSHAKE

2 frozen bananas, sliced
1 avocado, pitted and sliced
3 Tbsp raw cacao
2 cups plant-based milk
2 fresh dates, pitted

To think that something so simple can be so good. This one will have everyone (especially kids) asking for more!

Put it all in a blender and mix until you have a milkshake.

0,2

1 glass emits 0,2 kg/CO_2e

1 cake

BLACK BEAN BROWNIE

1 can (230g) cooked black beans
3 Tbsp cold pressed coconut oil
4 Tbsp unsweetened peanut butter
8 fresh dates, pitted
2 Tbsp water
¼ cup raw cacao
A pinch of salt

We know what you're thinking - Um, black beans and brownies don't go together!? - but trust us, they soooo do!

Rinse and drain the beans. Melt the coconut oil and peanut butter over low heat and then mix beans, dates, coconut oil, peanut butter and water in a food processor into a thick batter. Add the cacao and mix for another 20 seconds. Spread the batter evenly out in a parchment paper lined cake pan. Leave in the freezer for about 2 hours. Prepare the cake for a while before serving.

1,1

The whole cake emits 1,11 kg CO_2e

About 15 cookies

OAT COOKIES WITH CHOCOLATE

1 banana
2 cups oatmeal
1 dl light tahini
1 Tbsp raw cacao
a pinch of salt
4 squares dark chocolate (80%)

These wonderful little treats are sweetened with the banana. Green/unripe bananas contain more fiber than yellow-ripe bananas which provide a little more sweetness.

Preheat the oven to 100°C/225°F. Mash the banana and stir together with oats, tahini, cacao and salt. Place tablespoon-sized scoops on a baking sheet, pat down lightly and place a small piece of dark chocolate on top. Bake in the oven for 40 minutes.

0,3

A batch emits 0,27 kg/CO2e

| cake

CAKE x3

These fun cakes are somewhere between a brownie and a cake. You can use the same base with three different flavors to switch it out for the seasons. The classic is with chocolate flavor, the holiday one is with gingerbread seasonings and the elegant one is with saffron.

Base
3 eggs
15 fresh dates, pitted
1 ¼ cup almond flour
¼ cup water
2 Tbsp cold pressed coconut oil
1 tsp baking powder
A pinch of sea salt

Flavoring
¼ tsp (.5g) ground saffron
(replace dates with ½ cup of honey)
2 Tbsp gingerbread spices
3 Tbsp raw cacao

Preheat oven to 125°C/250°F. Grease a medium springform or tart mold with coconut oil. Mix all the base ingredients, plus your flavoring, together into a smooth batter in a food processor. Pour into the mold. Bake in the middle of the oven for 35 minutes, it's ok and even good if they are a little under baked like a gooey brownie.

1,0

A whole cake without flavoring emits 1,03 kg CO_2e

1 crisp

NUTRIENT HUNTER'S APPLE CRISP

1 ½ cup whole oat groats, soaked overnight (8 hrs)
1 cup rolled oats
10 fresh dates, pitted
½ tsp ground cardamom
1 tsp vanilla extract
6 apples
2 tsp ground cinnamon
1 Tbsp cold pressed canola oil

Garnish
vanilla "nice" cream
fresh lemon balm

When fall time rolls around you're going to want to remember this recipe! With apples and cinnamon nothing can go wrong.

Preheat the oven to 150°C /300°F. Drain the soaked oats well. Pulse the soaked oats in a food processor together with the rolled oats, dates, cardamom and vanilla into a crumble. Core and slice apples into wedges, combine with the cinnamon and canola oil and spread out in a baking dish. Spread the crumble over the apple wedges and bake in the oven until the apples are soft and the topping is crispy, about 45 mins. Best when served warm with a vanilla "nice" cream and chopped lemon balm.

0,4

Entire crisp emits 0,38 kg CO_2e

1 small bowl

A BOWL OF LICORICE

3 tsp licorice root powder
⅓ cup water
2 tsp sea salt
2 ½ cups almonds

You can't say you don't like black licorice until you've tried these almonds made with real licorice root powder. They are naturally sweet from the licorice and addictive with the combo of sea salt.

Pour the licorice powder, water and salt in a frying pan. Whisk together and bring to a simmer. Reduce the heat and add the almonds. Stir until the water has evaporated completely and the almonds are coated in the licorice. Pour onto a plate, sprinkle with a bit more salt and cool.

SCIENCE FOR YOU

Almonds crops require large quantities of water. And non-organic almond groves contribute to our vanishing bees. Eat almonds mindfully and buy organic!

0,5

One bowl emits 0,48 kg CO_2e

About 10 balls per sort

BLISS BALLS x3

Bliss balls are a great staple to keep in the freezer. That way if a real sweet tooth kicks in you can just take one out and enjoy it while also getting to fill in more circles in your compass.

BOUNTY BALLS

20 dried apricots
1 ¾ cups shredded coconut (unsweetened)
3 Tbsp cold pressed coconut oil
1 dark chocolate bar, at least 80%

These bounty balls are unbelievably good especially if you like the combo of coconut and chocolate.

Soak the apricots in warm water for 15 minutes and drain them. Add the apricots, coconut and coconut oil to a food processor and mix until it forms a dough. Roll into balls. Place in the freezer.

Melt the chocolate. Dip the balls in the chocolate and place them in the refrigerator or freezer until firm.

1,2

Entire batch emits 1,18 kg CO_2e

SNICKERS BALLS

½ can (115g) cooked chickpeas
½ cup unsweetened peanut butter
8 fresh dates, pitted
½ cup oatmeal
A pinch of salt
2 Tbsp cacao nibs

Garnish
raw cacao to roll in

The combination of chickpeas and peanut butter gives that cookie dough feeling that we all love. A bit like chocolate chip cookies - the nutrient hunter way!

Rinse and drain the chickpeas. Mix all ingredients except cocoa nibs into a smooth dough in a food processor. Add nibs and pulse a few times. Taste and adjust with more salt if needed. Allow to rest for 5 minutes before shaping into balls and rolling in cacao. Store in the fridge or freezer.

QUICK TIP!

On the days when you want a little extra luxury, skip the cacao and roll them in melted dark chocolate plus a pinch of sea salt on top.

0,3

Entire batch emits 0,33 kg/CO_2e

BLUEBERRY BALLS

1 cup frozen blueberries
1 cup cashews, soaked 1–4 hrs
1 cup shredded coconut
1 tsp ground cardamom
1 tsp vanilla

Garnish
¼ cup dried blueberry powder to roll in

We'll admit it, this recipe does seem a bit unusual at first glance but we really hope you try it because they are also unusually good!

Run everything in a food processor until the dough holds together, roll into balls and then into blueberry powder. Eat directly or store in the fridge or freezer. They may need to thaw slightly if they have been in the freezer.

VARIATION!

Try replacing the blueberries with raspberries or strawberries. Or a blend of berries!

1,0

Entire batch emits 0,97 kg/CO_2e

8 small ice creams

FOOD PHARMACY'S ICE CREAM

Ice cream

1 cup cashews, soaked 2-4 hrs
1 cup coconut milk or
plant-based cream
10 fresh dates, pitted
1 tsp vanilla
A pinch of sea salt
2 Tbsp cold coffee
1 bar dark chocolate, at least 80%

Garnish ideas

freeze-dried berries
cacao nibs
shredded coconut
melted chocolate
chopped nuts or seeds
sea salt

Hold on to your hats because this recipe is going to blow you away. So creamy, so decadent and very yummy! Dip them in dark chocolate after freezing and go crazy with garnish. We used small silicone ice cream forms to make ours.

Drain and rinse the cashews. Mix the cashews in a blender with coconut milk, dates, vanilla, salt and cold coffee. Run until you have a smooth cream. Fill 8 ice cream molds with the ice cream batter. Place in the freezer until firm.

Melt the chocolate but let it cool slightly. Remove the ice cream from the freezer molds, dip each one in the melted chocolate and sprinkle immediately with garnish. Place them on a plate with parchment paper and return to the freezer to harden before serving. Store in the freezer.

<0,1

A ice cream emits 0,1 kg CO_2e

12 squares

ALMOND COOKIE BARS WITH BERRIES

Bars

1 can (230g) cooked white beans
1 ½ tsp baking powder
¼ cup almond butter
½ cup plant-based milk
½ cup oatmeal
½ cup almond flour
5 bitter almonds (or 3 drops almond extract)
½ tsp of vanilla
12 fresh dates, pitted
¼ tsp sea salt
¼ cup frozen or fresh berries (lingonberry, raspberry, etc)

Garnish

fresh berries or in season fruits with fresh lemon balm

Chewy cookie bars with a secret ingredient (don't let skeptics know this): white beans!

Preheat oven to 150°C/300°F. Strain and rinse the beans. Finely grate the bitter almonds.

Mix all ingredients to a completely smooth batter in a food processor. Line a small baking dish with parchment paper. Pour the batter into the baking dish and sprinkle with the berries. Bake in the middle of the oven for 75-90 minutes, until the cake is set and has a slight golden crust. Allow it to cool before cutting into squares. Garnish with more fresh berries or fruit and some lemon balm.

0,5

One batch emits 0,46 kg CO_2e

CLOSING MEDITATION

Before we release you back into the wilderness with all of your new found nutrient hunter tools, we want you to stay put for one last closing meditation. Making a habit out of being thankful spurs positivity. Hopefully you've made a habit out of thanking your body for being there for you just like we taught you at the beginning of this book - as well as the planet for everything it provides. This time though, we want you to close your eyes and spend a moment thinking about who else in your life you are thankful for.

Take it at your own pace and let the names come to you. In writing the conclusion of this book, we think of Anna Lindelöw Mannheimer, Ann Fernholm, Elin Röös, Martin Brunnberg, Fredrik Paulún, Ulrika Ekblom, Cecilia Viklund, Linnéa von Zweigbergk, Cicki Foconi, Louise Sjöholm, father Janne, mother Ann, Ninni, Ludde, Carl, June, Emil , Rajraj, Pyret, Taxi, Filippa, Jonna, Katja, Sebbe, Frida, Carbon Cloud for their climate calculations, Lisa Eckerström for the brownie recipe with black beans, our beloved followers and all of you who came into our office this past year to cut your hair (because you were looking for the hair studio one door over).

And last but not least - a big thank you to those of you who took the time to read this book and have just graduated to a full-fledged Nutrient Hunter!

REGISTER

KATEGORIREGISTER